State Constitutional Convention Studies
Number Five

WITH AN
UNDERSTANDING HEART:
Constitution Making in Hawaii

NORMAN MELLER
University of Hawaii

D1468546

NATIONAL MUNICIPAL LEAGUE
Carl H. Pforzheimer Building
47 East 68 Street, New York, New York 10021

1971

Cover: Iolani Palace seen from the new state Capitol. The constitutions drafted by both the 1950 and 1968 conventions were signed in the throne room of the Palace.

Foreword

All previous publications in this series on constitutional conventions deal with states where nineteenth-century constitutions imposed out-dated structures and procedures. Constitutional antecedents in the fiftieth state also go back to the mid-nineteenth century and the constitutions of the Hawaiian monarchy and independent republic, but this study by Norman Meller concentrates on the 1968 convention and systematically compares it with the 1950 convention which drafted Hawaii's statehood constitution. The products of both conventions were approved by the voters, which means that the reader from another state should be sensi-tive to elements which led to victory at the polls. The author notes, how-ever, that both conventions "were disposed toward minimal, incremental change," which suggests that these experiences may have deficiencies for states whose basic law requires fundamental change.

Preparation for constitutional revision by convention or otherwise is fre-quently crucial to the success of the undertaking. The pre-1950 conven-tion effort was a part of the overall strategy for achieving statehood, but that preceding the 1968 convention involved an unusual combination of activities which greatly increased citizen understanding of state gov-ernment and helped prepare the delegates for their responsibilities. Re-lated to the pre-convention educational efforts was the role of the media in all phases of the process. Press, radio and TV were strongly committed

iii

to the "good government" position, but, according to the author, neglected the negative aspects of the convention.

An issue which has received increased attention following the defeat of revised constitutions in several states is the method of presenting the recommendations of a convention to the voters—in a single package or in the form of separate propositions. The 1968 Hawaiian Convention utilized a unique combination of the two approaches. Perhaps the "yes-no; yes-but" ballot is peculiarly suited to the revision of a basically modern constitution where dividing up the package is not a draftsman's nightmare, but some other states may want to consider the possibility of using it.

Dr. Meller states that he is recording only "one person's observations," but it should be added that his impressions have special significance because of his intimate familiarity with the developments in Hawaii since he became director of the Legislative Reference Bureau in 1947 shortly before it undertook the background research for the 1950 convention. As professor of political science at the University of Hawaii since 1955, he has been both participant and observer in governmental processes during the years immediately before and after statehood.

A grant from the Carnegie Corporation of New York made this study possible. The statements and views expressed are solely the responsibility of the author.

WILLIAM N. CASSELLA, JR.
Executive Director

March 1971

Preface

The following pages record one person's observations on constitution making in Hawaii. They are based on participation in the manipulative buildup of community interest in the institution of constitutional drafting; the preparation of basic source materials for convention delegates' use; attendance at countless committee and plenary sessions; numerous informal discussions with delegates, convention staff and reporters of newspapers, radio and television; and a running check on the content of the mass media's reporting on the progress of Hawaii's constitutional efforts. This mustering of data in comparative fashion for Hawaii's two state constitutional conventions is intended to be neither exhaustive in detail nor statistically precise; these are the functions of another study on state constitution making being conducted under other auspices. In short, it is one man's impressions, hopefully useful as an accurate description of fact and provocative in encouraging further research as well as rethinking the role of the constitutional convention.

NORMAN MELLER

Table of Contents

1.

Hawaii

We, the people of the State of Hawaii . . . with an understanding heart toward all the peoples of the earth, do hereby ordain and establish this constitution. —*Preamble, Constitution 1950. Retained by Convention, 1968.*

Hawaii is a land of many contrasts, no less so in constitution making which has been reoccurring for over a century. Although admitted as a state only 12 years ago, twice in the last 20 years, Hawaiians have elected delegates to constitutional conventions. Later the voters adopted those conventions' handiwork as the Islands' state constitution. This is an account of Hawaii's most recent constitutional experiences, the constitutional convention of 1968, with perspective furnished by reference to the efforts of 1950, and antecedents stretching far back. The earliest Hawaiian constitution was in 1840, followed by three monarchical constitutions, the 1894 constituent document of the republic which overthrew the Monarchy when the last Queen had the misguided judgment to attempt promulgation of her own constitution, and, finally, the Organic Act adopted by the Congress of the United States which served basically as the territory's constitution for over half a century.

Constitution making, like other acts of lawmaking, embodies as well as reflects the play of the formative forces which contribute to shaping the final product. History plays an important role in the canalizing of those forces, even if no more than to proffer a too easy precedent to follow. Hawaii's refurbished 1968 constitution is an amended version of that

1

adopted in 1950. The drafting of the latter was in good part conditioned by the Islands' experiences with the workings of the territory's Organic Act, just as each of the earlier documents relied somewhat on those that preceded it. Notwithstanding this heritage, which helps to relate the substantive nuances and variations of the Islands' constitutions with the long history of development under a succession of South Seas political regimes, as well as with unique geography, demography and an island economy, the process of preparing Hawaii's state constitutions falls squarely within the central stream of constitution making in the United States, and can be studied as such.

Geographic, Demographic and Economic Characteristics

In 1950, when the delegates met to draft a constitution for the proposed state of Hawaii, the census numbered about 500,000 people on the Islands' approximately 6,400 square miles. Small as these statistics showed Hawaii to be, some satisfaction could be found in the knowledge that three states were smaller in area and four in population, and at least nine paid less taxes into the federal treasury. Hawaii as a republic had been considerably less populated, so that the 1950 number represented more than a doubling during the 50 years of territorial status; its citizenship component had increased almost six times, and its registered voters nearly 12.

No single ethnic group constituted a majority, but, unlike any area on the mainland, persons of Oriental ancestry predominated in numbers, with the Japanese the largest single unit. Nearly 14 percent of Hawaii's people were then aliens. The many minority strains had been woven into an unusual composite by virtue of cross-marriage, and the contiguity of daily living and working relationships had developed a culture in which American precepts of government had long been accepted and internalized, ready to be expressed in the drafting of a state constitution.

Population was unevenly distributed over Hawaii's four units of local government, with 70 percent reported on Oahu, the island which is practically coterminous with the city and county of Honolulu. Despite Honolulu being the capital of the territory, and its commercial and business center, much of its land was devoted to agriculture, which was still the foundation of Hawaii's economy, the greatest influence, of course, being sugar and pineapple—with their plantations, canneries, factories and interrelated institutions. Rephrased in ethnic terms, this meant that *haoles* (Caucasians of north European ancestry) occupied the key economic positions. Primarily through the Republican party, some of these same men also played a comparable role in shaping major political decisions, while that party had controlled both houses of the territorial legislature for nearly half a century.

By the time of the second constitutional convention in 1968 not even the statistic on land area remained unchanged. Statehood had removed outlying islands from Hawaii's jurisdiction, which in effect reduced the size of the city and county of Honolulu. Population had markedly increased to just shy of 800,000, and Oahu's imbalance had reached over 80 percent of the total. The inflow of residents from the mainland resulted in the Caucasians supplanting the Japanese as the largest single component. The total number of registered voters had increased almost 50 percent since the first statehood election.

Corporate agriculture, while still large, was now eclipsed by tourism, and federal expenditures brought more money into the Island economy than both. The economic dominance of the old Island power structure was successfully challenged and pretty much fractionated by the massive entry of mainland-based enterprise and the emergence of centers of economic power from the Islands' rapidly growing middle class. Hawaii's major labor union, the International Longshoremen's and Warehousemen's Union (ILWU), had shed its radical image and the fear of internal Communist subversion had about disappeared. All this was accompanied with the transference of the formal political trappings of power, and since 1955 the Democratic party had enjoyed sizable majorities in both houses of the legislature and elected its members to most offices of local government.

The manner in which the delegates to the 1950 convention turned to their duties, and the provisions ultimately included in that constitution were materially influenced by the conditions prevailing at the time. But they were not the sole determinants, just as the changed conditions of 1968 did not automatically result in any massive reshaping of the original document. The heritage of history also helped to illuminate the provisions of both. And it is too simplistic to treat the delegates as disregarding their own values and prejudices, and responding mechanically in a behavioristic way to the net total of political forces impinging on them. All of these diverse factors contributed to the final form of the constitutional provisions submitted for public referendum, with the prevailing situation at best the proximate cause for convening the constitutional convention.

Statehood and the 1950 Constitutional Convention

The reasons for undertaking the painstaking chore of constitution drafting in 1950 differed significantly from those of 1968. Hawaii in 1950 did not conceive of the constitution as an end in itself, but only as a means, as part of the greater, organized effort to achieve statehood. Once drafted and approved at the polls, it would remain a propaganda gesture until the federal Congress accepted Hawaii into the Union of states and thereby gave it legal life.

This drive to statehood did not originate with constitution making, for its beginnings may be traced back as early as 1903 when a joint resolution of the territorial legislature petitioned for admission. After World War I, with increase in statehood interest, enabling legislation was repeatedly introduced in the federal Congress, only to die in committee. The first congressional visits to Hawaii on the statehood question started in 1935. After World War II, the tempo of the campaign quickened, with expensive educational campaigns mounted from Hawaii, and an office of the Hawaii Statehood Commission maintained in Washington to keep contact with the Congress. The unilateral drafting of a state constitution without prior congressional consent and then its presentation to Washington as a *fait accompli* was adopted as a strategic gamble in 1949 as an alternative to the more conventional approach of seeking enabling legislation.

In choosing to prepare a "hope chest" constitution, Hawaii was not setting out on an uncharted path, for 15 states had held conventions prior to the granting of congressional consent. Congressional concurrence was in no way certain, however. Hawaii's lack of contiguity with the continental United States, relatively miniscule size, polyglot population, unique political past and reputedly Communist-led labor all contributed to mainlanders' suspicions regarding the loyalty of Hawaii's people and their capacity to govern themselves as a co-equal state. These qualms were also shared by a minority of Islanders, who for a variety of reasons did not favor an immediate grant of statehood: a plebiscite conducted in 1940 showed a third of Hawaii's voters were opposed. The drafting of Hawaii's "hope chest" constitution was deliberately undertaken as a double-edged ploy, as a demonstration to mainland doubters that the people of the Islands would undertake their own governance in a mature manner, and to reassure doubting Islanders that the government proposed for Hawaii would so protect them that they could safely throw in their lot with statehood. As the most ambitious promotion up to that time in a broad-ranging and well-financed public relations program, the purely manipulative objective underlying the calling of Hawaii's first state constitutional convention now tends to be buried in the euphoria of statehood achieved.

The manner in which Hawaii's people participated in selecting the delegates was looked on as an assist, but, at the same time, it could potentially raise an obstruction to statehood. The Congress could be favorably impressed by sheer statistics: the number of citizens who registered to vote at the constitutional elections, the candidates who presented themselves for election, and the size of voter turnout at the polls. Skimpiness in any of these would be interpreted in Washington as proof that Hawaii's people had little interest in changing the territorial status. Near complete involvement was tantamount to enthusiastic endorsement of statehood. And other dangers had to be guarded against: "plunking" when voting for candidates should be avoided for it would lead to the suspicion of racial bloc voting, and this in turn would give ammunition to statehood's enemies.

But all turned out well; registration figures were high, there were contests for all delegate posts, and the slightly smaller than normal percentage of voters who turned out at the polls could be explained away without hurting the statehood cause. Of momentarily greater import, of the 14 candidates endorsed by the ILWU, only two won and one was later expelled from the convention. If further demonstration of the Islanders' dedication to American principles was needed, it was later furnished by the contents of the constitution drafted by the delegates, who fittingly ended their historic chores in the name-signing ceremony by singing the "Star Spangled Banner." The constitution was ratified by a vote of better than three to one, despite the ILWU leaders' strong opposition. This "conservative" state constitution which they attacked included the controversial provision, found in no other constituent document, that "no person who advocates, or who aids or belongs to any party, organization or association which advocates the overthrow by force or violence of the government of this state or of the United States shall be qualified to hold any public office or employment." The new Hawaiian constitution thus nicely served its intended functions, as Exhibit A to demonstrate Hawaii's maturity and security for the statehood cause in Washington, and as a device to aggregate and articulate the Islanders' desires to the same end. Coincidentally, the delegates had succeeded in drafting a document which, in the encomium of the National Municipal League, "set a new high standard in the writing of a modern state constitution by a convention."

Reapportionment and the 1968 Constitutional Convention

With Hawaii's constitutional convention in 1950 attributable to political expediency in furtherance of the statehood cause, similarly the one held in 1968 may be traced to political ineptitude. Neither the major leadership of the Democratic party nor the ILWU—the most potent pressure group in the Islands—originally favored calling the convention, and its convening in July 1968 occurred only through a series of events which gradually assumed an inexorable momentum precluding all attempts at delay.

The background of the 1968 convention might be said to begin when the reapportionment formula of the Hawaiian legislature specified in the constitution of 1950 ran afoul of the "one man, one vote" doctrine enunciated by the U. S. Supreme Court. In 1964, three weeks after the Supreme Court decision in *Reynolds* v. *Sims,* Hawaii's attorney general submitted a series of opinions to the governor concluding that apportionment of both the Senate and the House violated the equal protection clause of the federal constitution as now interpreted by the court. He also held that the legislature had authority to enact a statute for apportionment on a temporary as well as a permanent basis, and recommended that a special session be called immediately to implement the Supreme Court's decision. Meanwhile a friendly test case would be brought to set aside the existing reapportionment provisions in the state constitution.

The legislators duly convened in special session. The major bills introduced, at the behest of Governor John A. Burns, called for a reapportionment of both houses to go into effect immediately without prior popular approval. The people would later be afforded an opportunity to vote for the constitutional amendment proposing the same plan. The cumulative effect of the administration measures would have been to strengthen the governor's political position as leader of the state's majority party. Perhaps because of this the two houses could not concur on either the substance or the procedure of reapportionment, and the special session ended disastrously.

After the federal district court, early in 1965, found the apportionment of Hawaii's Senate invalid, as well as some of the reapportionment provisions in the state constitution, it directed that the constitutional route be followed in correcting the malapportionment and filling the hiatus left in the constitution. To make doubly sure that all of this would be resolved before the 1966 legislative elections, the court set up a specific timetable for placing on the ballot the question, "Shall there be a convention to propose a revision of or amendments to the constitution?"

Final adoption of all other legislation by the Hawaiian legislature was foreclosed by court order until a bill was enacted calling the constitutional convention.

Neither the legislature nor the governor was willing to accede to the court's direction. As an alternative the legislature petitioned and received permission from the court to adopt a provisional reapportionment and redistricting plan, and meanwhile get on with its legislative work. As part of the plan the legislature included a measure which would give the people an opportunity to approve the temporary reapportionment in the form of a constitutional amendment and another bill permitting the voters to indicate whether or not they desired a constitutional convention to be convened. The court rejected the reappointment plan and some legislators assumed that the rejection invalidated all three bills. The measure putting the question of calling a constitutional convention on the ballot was considered as duly passed, however, and was processed accordingly by the staff. Eventually, on appeal, the U. S. Supreme Court in *Burns* v. *Richardson** unanimously upheld the legislative proposal as a temporary reapportionment and, while not requiring it, appeared to take for granted a constitutional convention as necessary for implementing a permanent plan.

Some legislators now saw the approved temporary plan as the basis for permanent reapportionment through the route of constitutional amendment, without need for calling a convention with its attendant risks. If the constitutional convention question could be removed from the 1966 ballot through action of a special session, they argued, it would still have to come before the electorate automatically in 1968 or 1970 under Hawaii's constitutional mandate for a decennial vote on the issue. Other legislators proposed adoption of a constitutional amendment which would make the temporary interim reapportionment the final plan, and at the same time urge the voters to defeat the constitutional convention question which would be kept on the ballot. This would have deferred a convention for another decade. Unfortunately, however, memory of the negative 1964 special session, the diversity of positions being advocated by Hawaii's political leaders, and the charge that all of the maneuvering was an immoral scheme to bypass the electorate, cumulatively contributed to a state of stasis. While various individuals plotted and publicly proposed, like a Greek tragedy, the election date drew ever closer. In

---

* For a full consideration of Hawaii's reapportionment before the courts, see chapter by author in Eleanore Bushnell, ed., *Impact of Reapportionment on the Western States* (Salt Lake City: University of Utah Press, 1970).

November 1966, Hawaii's voters went to the polls and both elected legislators under the temporary reapportionment plan and affirmatively sanc-
tioned the holding of a constitutional convention.

Any attempt to delay necessary implementing legislation at the 1967
regular session, regardless of the governor's and legislative leaders' view
on the need for that convention, would now be politically ill-advised. A
polling of the candidates during the legislative election in 1966 indicated
that 90 percent of those responding (149 candidates, 125 responses)
favored a convention, and that about half of them also would support a
special election for the choosing of convention delegates. Later, they
honored these expressed views, but, by setting the convening of the convention close to the 1968 primary election, the means adopted for implementation demonstrated that they desired the convention delegates to
tend quickly to a few major issues and then adjourn. The legislature also
made provision for placing the court-ordered "temporary" reapportionment on the 1968 general election ballot in the form of a constitutional
amendment. It could always be urged as a substitute for the constitutional convention's proposal should the latter threaten to disturb the new
balance of representation laboriously worked out by the legislature.
Since the voters wanted a constitutional convention they would have one,
but under limitations fixed by the legislature.

Limitations on the Conventions

The delegates to both the 1950 and the 1968 conventions operated
under constraint. At the former, everything they did as well as did not
do would be subjected to the harsh scrutiny of public opinion, and, more
specifically, that of the congressmen on whose key votes statehood de-
pended.

The 1968 convention delegates were similarly fettered, although the
limitations under which they served were internal. The convention was
called against objections that reapportionment was the only urgent constitutional problem facing the state, and this could be handled more
quickly and efficiently by the legislature. When they convened, a large
contingent of delegates was impatient to take to the hustings to seek
election to the legislature or other office. The prevailing spirit, from the
pre-convening caucuses onward, was to denigrate efforts at slowing down
the thrust of convention business and opening up fundamental matters
to careful and considered review.

Many of the provisions of the Organic Act were directly or by in-
ference incorporated into the 1950 "hope chest" constitution. This

helped reinforce the image of Hawaii as safe and mature. Now, two decades later, the opportunity was offered to reexamine the document, and to confirm or reject its contents free of the legal, political and psychological pressures attending statehood. Even if they were so inclined, the delegates to the 1968 convention were not permitted sufficient time to undertake any such fundamental reconsideration. But, then again, Hawaii's constitution had been extravagantly praised, and most of the delegates were not of a mind to question that judgment.

By way of an epilogue to the parallelism of the conventions, both functioned under the frowns of Hawaii's governors. Territorial Governor Ingram M. Stainbach was reputedly "lukewarm" to immediate statehood and was carried more by the current of the times. Governor Burns, in unequivocal terms, indicated his disapproval of having a convention meet in 1968. Once the people voted affirmatively on the question his attitude became one of "it's what the people want" and he resigned himself to a convention. At no time did he express interest in the delegates taking on more than reapportionment and debt ceiling changes, and possibly a few other issues which could be rapidly resolved.

2.

Convention Size and Districting

The process of districting a constitutional convention is inevitably influenced by the decisions previously incorporated into the structuring of the state legislature. On the more mechanical level of linkage, the building blocks with which the constitutional convention districts are normally constructed are the basic unit of the legislative district, with their personal and party precinct organizations erected to muster voters' support. On the more conceptual level, attitudes toward multi-member or single-member districting in the convention, to over- or under-representation of specific areas, and to comparable other matters, have all been conditioned by the practices observed in districting the state legislature. Preparing the structure of Hawaii's state conventions proved no exception, and the size of the convention, the districting configuration, and the allocation of delegates among the districts all had legislative antecedents.

Ever since the first legislature began functioning during the days of the Monarchy, Hawaii has had multi-member districting. Since annexation, the Neighbor Islands (Hawaii, Maui and Kauai) had been increasingly over-represented in the territorial legislature vis-à-vis the bulk of the population residing on Oahu. With a 15-member Senate and a House of Representatives double that size, the convention had to be at least large enough to accommodate all members of the territorial legislature, with districts so spaced that incumbent legislators could run as delegates without having to compete. These were the realities to be faced in setting the size and in working out the apportionment system for the 1950 constitutional convention.

The territorial act which called for the convening of the convention apportioned 63 delegates among the counties so that 27 were allocated to the Neighbor Islands—Hawaii, 12; Maui, nine; and Kauai, six—and the remaining 36 to the city and county of Honolulu. One-third of the delegates were elected at large, running from the existing six representative districts, and two-thirds were chosen from smaller groupings of precincts into which each of those districts was divided. But how did the territorial legislators agree on the magic figure of 63?

1950: Size and Districting

For the 1950 convention each of the three Neighbor Island counties received as many delegates as it had members in the legislature. In each the number of delegates who ran at large was equal to the number of its senators, and the balance sought election from combinations of precincts grouped within the various representative districts. The share of its seats in the legislature was doubled for the city and county of Honolulu, in recognition of its greater population, and the 12 at-large delegates similarly represented double the number of its territorial senators. All this constituted a compromise reached several years earlier by a subcommittee of the Citizens Statehood Committee, and had been incorporated into the statehood enabling bill passed by the U. S. House of Representatives in 1947, which thereafter languished and then died in the U. S. Senate. A few minor amendments in 1948 adjusted the apportionment to reflect the creation of several new precincts, and it was again included in the enabling measures introduced into the Congress in 1949. The 1949 territorial legislature merely copied the terminology in the pending statehood legislation.

The strategy of using the compromise in the statehood bill was urged by the Republican majority in the territorial legislature. The Democrats introduced an alternative plan, calling for a convention of 129 delegates, which would have given Oahu a much larger majority of the convention (82). Their proposal was also tied to the existing legislative districts, so that it did not interject a different basis for determining the convention's structure. All of the plans made provision for smaller, precinct groupings within the legislative, at-large delegate election districts, a bifurcation intended to ensure representation in the convention for every area and to give newcomers to politics a better chance of winning their contests.

The Republican plan won out, probably not too surprising given the Republican composition of the legislature, although the statehood movement was bipartisan. Later, during the campaign on Oahu for election of delegates, the Democratic county chairman (presently Hawaii's governor) charged that the small, grouped-precinct districts had been arranged by the Republicans to favor their own party's candidates. Be that as it may, there is no question but that equality of representation was not obtained in the 1950 effort to fit the convention within the prevailing legislative districting.

By 1967 the formula for apportionment of delegates used in the 1950 convention appeared to have lost all utility, this notwithstanding the constitutional provision that "unless the legislature shall otherwise provide, there shall be the same number of delegates to . . . [the] convention, who shall be elected from the same areas . . . as nearly as practicable, as required for the Hawaii State Constitutional Convention of 1950." For one thing the legislature had been enlarged to 76 members, and the number of representative districts had been increased to 18. Of greater import, the weight of representation in both houses had now shifted more in favor of Oahu. Assuming, without conceding, that the reapportionment cases applied to the districting of a constitutional convention, the new body would have to be more heavily weighted for Honolulu city and county delegates. And, finally, when it came time to draw the actual lines for the delegate districts it would be Democratic majorities in both houses of the legislature which would be in position to favor potential candidates.

1968: Size and Districting

It was again the responsibility of the Hawaiian legislature to fix the size and districting of the 1968 convention. What ensued can best be explained within the frame of bitter inter-house competition, with the final determination to increase the convention size to exceed that of the legislature reached in a conference committee's photo-finish compromise on the last day of the session. Initially the House proposal set up districts identical to the existing 18 representative districts, and the same number of delegates (51) as representatives. The Senate's measure was tied to senatorial districts and the convention's size (50) was double that of the Senate. The objections voiced by concerned individuals and organizations, supported by the major daily newspapers, assured that neither could be enacted without major alteration. Provision would have to be made for the non-political aspects of the convention, permitting the neophyte some chance of success against the legislative candidate with his organization of campaign workers, long-established alliances and political party support.

The House of Representatives fixed the final figure of 82 delegates as the size for the convention, a number selected as the result of an apportionment designed to afford "meaningful and effective representation" on roughly the basis of 3,000 registered voters per delegate. At the 1950 convention the ratio had approximated 2,243 to one, but if this were to be duplicated in 1968 with Hawaii's expanded population it would have necessitated a convention of 113 delegates. Sixty-three, the number in 1950, was too small to accommodate the enlarged legislature; 113 was termed unwieldy; 82 was seized on as defensible and, as a compromise, embodied all of the concessions which comprise a bargaining-type decision. The "historical, geographical and political distinctiveness" of the first representative district on the island of Hawaii could be maintained, even though it had only 2,369 registered voters. Similarly, the fourth district on the same island would have to be content with only one delegate, even though it had almost double the number of registered voters (4,344). The Neighbor Islands, collectively, might have fewer delegates in 1968 than in 1950, but, with the larger convention, in no case would the reduction be more than one-third. In any case the number of delegates proposed and the way districts were drawn permitted all interested incumbent legislators to seek delegate posts without necessity of any competing for the same seat.

One of the key decisions was the determination of the number of delegates to be elected at large. In 1950, two-thirds of the delegates were elected from small districts composed of combined precincts, each formed within one of the six representative districts. In 1968, less than a majority of delegates came from these smaller districts. For one thing Hawaii now had 18 representative districts, which permitted less opportunity, after providing for the at-large candidates, also to divide the representative districts. Even where the possibility existed, Hawaii's legislators were not overly anxious to set up these smaller delegate districts. As a result, for the 1968 convention there were 46 delegates at large and only 36 from districts composed of combined precincts within a representative district. As seven at-large districts each elected only one delegate, for the 1968 constitutional convention there were in all 43 single-member districts. The rest of the 39 delegates came from 11 multi-member districts, 33 of them from Oahu.

In 1950, when the provisions of Hawaii's "hope chest" constitution were before the convention's Committee of the Whole, an amendment

COMPOSITION OF 1950 AND 1968 CONVENTIONS COMPARED

	1950	1968
Delegates	63	82
Neighbor Islands	27	19
	(43%)	(23%)
Honolulu	36	63
	(57%)	(77%)
At-large Districts	6	18
no. of delegates	21	46
(delegates % of total)	(33%)	(56%)
Grouped-precincts Districts	30	36
no. of delegates	42	36
(delegates % of total)	(67%)	(44%)
Single-member Districts	18	43
no. of delegates	18	43
(delegates % of total)	(29%)	(52%)

had been proposed to have future conventions consist of the same number of delegates as representatives and senators in the state legislature, and be elected in a similar manner. The effect of the amendment would have been to set up legislative districting and partisan elections for constitutional conventions. The amendment was defeated but the 1967 legislature ignored this and initially proceeded as if it were to be the guiding standard. In the bills as introduced, delegates were to be elected at large from legislative districts; partisan elections would replace the nonpartisan approach used for the 1950 convention; as in the legislature, the member elected from the first representative district would be temporary chairman; a statutory adjournment date would be fixed for the convention subject to the legislative grant of an extension; and the salaries and allowances of delegates would be the same as currently received by legislators. The changes introduced during the course of the legislation's passage through both houses helped return a more *sui generis* character to the convention. In addition to modifying the districting, reference to partisan elections was removed and, at least nominally, the duration was left to convention determination. Whether the 1950 experience should be duplicated with both primary and final elections, or a single election substituted, remained a matter of contention between the two houses to the very end of the session. The Senate's position won out, on the grounds that a single election would not only save the taxpayers unnecessary expenses but would also enable political neophytes to seek election without incurring unreasonable campaign costs.

On a number of occasions the committees considering convention legislation indicated in their reports that their decisions were designed to facilitate the candidacy of the political newcomer. As already noted, this was the reputed reason for telescoping the primary and final elections into one. The large number of single-member districts was believed by the House Judiciary Committee to "not only neutralize the advantage enjoyed by the legislators, but also help those less able to afford large-scale campaigns." On balance, however, the weight of decisions pushed the scale to aiding the incumbent legislator if he wished to run, and to continue him longer in his legislative seat if he did not. To the latter end the date for the convening of the convention was set for July 15, 1968, too late for the convention to complete its work in time for a hurried special election. All of the hold-over senators thus faced no risk of finding themselves required to run again in 1968, cutting in half their four-year terms. When legislators announced their candidacy as delegates, and availed themselves of the campaign organization inherited from previous election contests in their home territory, it became readily apparent that the size and districting of the 1968 convention was to their advantage. This was particularly evident when 24 (almost one-third of the total legislature) opted for candidacy from single-member districts. The districting of the 1950 convention had successfully used the grid of the then existing legislative apportionment without the convention being captured by incumbent legislators; the repetition of the practice for the 1968 convention, but now with that body not much larger than the size of the legislature, subjected it to the risk of domination by legislators.

3.

"Tooling Up" the Community

Two of the final areas of contention between the houses of Hawaii's legislature in agreeing to call the 1968 constitutional convention were over scheduling the election for delegates and the convening date of the convention. Witnesses testified to the need for structuring community interest in holding the convention, and educating both citizen and delegate on the issues which might be raised. Newspaper comment favored delaying the convention long enough to allow an educational buildup prior to the election of delegates and, thereafter, a sufficient amount of time to permit the delegates to brief themselves before convention deliberations began. One of the justifications for eliminating the primary election was to provide money to pay the cost of advertisements covering the issues and presenting the qualifications of the candidates.

As finally adopted, a year would elapse before the special election, and $100,000 was appropriated "to the office of the Governor, or to the Lieutenant Governor, if so designated by the Governor, for the arrangement and purchase of advertising in the general media to cover, on an equal and fair basis, the issues involved or likely to be involved in the convention, and in addition thereto to do such things as he may consider necessary to focus the public's attention on the importance of the constitutional convention." In addition, $20,000 was appropriated for the Legislative Reference Bureau of the University of Hawaii to hire personnel necessary to update the 1950 manual on state constitutional provisions "and to prepare necessary reports for the convention." All this was in sharp contrast with the financially straitened "tooling up" operation which preceded the convening of Hawaii's first constitutional convention in 1950.

1950: Pre-Convention Work

As early as 1947 the Statehood Commission had anticipated the need for undertaking steps supportive to the writing of a state constitution. In September of that year, a 24-member committee of prominent political figures was appointed to conduct a study of state constitutions. The staff of the university's Legislative Reference Bureau served as its research arm. The group divided into six subcommittees, their areas of study patterned after the division of work followed by the subcommittees of the New York State Constitutional Convention Commission a decade earlier. Complying with the charge to implement the groundwork for a constitutional convention, to clarify public opinion on the various provisions needed to be incorporated in a state constitution, and to submit tentative constitutional provisions for public discussion prior to the election of convention delegates, the subcommittees met periodically for nearly two years. Most of their recommendations were not reached until early in 1950, just prior to the primary election for delegates. When released, they were widely reported in the newspapers and helped to promote public discussion of constitutional issues during the election campaign. A number of the committee members ran as delegates, and some were successful at the polls. Evidencing the minimal budget allocated, copies of the subcommittee reports were mimeographed and hand-stapled by the Statehood Commission staff for public dissemination.

The research conducted by the Legislative Reference Bureau served a dual purpose. It also became the source for the 396-page, 1950 manual on state constitutional provisions compiled by the bureau for the constitutional convention. The cost of its printing was borne by the Statehood Commission, and it, too, was issued in simple format and offset at minimal cost.

A second group which helped early to lay the community foundations for this first state convention was comprised of 63 University of Hawaii students. They were elected by the student body in 1948 to a model state constitutional convention from the same geographical districts as the convention delegates in 1950. Sworn in by the chief justice of the territorial supreme court, they organized themselves, adopted rules of procedure, established committees, and, after debating at length, drafted a model state constitution. The interest of the general community in the

students' deliberations was kindled by front-page newspaper stories reporting their activities. The two-months' work of the student group was
published in a modest pamphlet for general distribution.

Educating the public on constitutional issues and the mechanics of
holding a constitutional convention in 1950 was a decentralized and dis-
persed undertaking to which the efforts of the Statehood Commission,
the political parties and the press were major contributors. Other existing community organizations—religious, patriotic, business, youth and educational—sponsored a variety of activities to acquaint their own members and the general public with both convention candidates and likely
issues. As the campaign built up to its peak prior to the primary, and
then later for the runoff election, these organizations invited convention
candidates to address their members, either on behalf of their own
candidacy or on the general subject of writing a state constitution. To the
extent that there was any coordination underlying this effort, it was supplied by the small staff of the Statehood Commission. In comparison
with the government-financed, preparatory work preceding the 1968
constitutional convention, it must be charitably scored as sincerely intended but somewhat amateurish.

1968: Pre-Convention Work

Almost a year prior to the convening of the 1968 constitutional convention, pursuant to a single-house resolution, the Senate president appointed
an Advisory Committee on the Legislative Process to make recommendations on legislative improvement. The speaker of the House concurred
in the appointments, fully understanding that the committee's study and
proposals would eventually find their way to the constitutional convention floor. The blue-ribbon committee also was aware that its function
was not limited to non-constitutional matters. Among its recommendations it included annual legislative sessions, carryover of bills between
sessions, automatic pay raises for legislators, changes in length of terms
and major modifications in legislative representation, all of which necessitated constitutional amendment.

Many of the other recommendations could be accomplished through
modifying the legislative rules, but all were held in abeyance by the
1968 legislature which received the committee's report. With tongue-in-
cheek, the Citizens Conference on State Legislatures noted that the
forthcoming constitutional convention in Hawaii would undoubtedly review the legislative article of the constitution, and added "since many of

the committee's recommendations would require constitutional revision, the timing is extremely fortunate."

Much closer to the election date, various organized groups in the state began advocating specific modifications in the constitution as well as developing defense strategies aimed at deterring amendments of which they disapproved. A Citizens' Committee on Ethics in Government formulated a proposal for a constitutional article. The Tax Foundation of Hawaii distributed reports on the principal arguments for and against either annual or biennial budget systems, and other subjects for constitutional revision. But by far the greatest organized, educational effort was conducted by two separate and disparate committees.

There are two classical methods of preparation for a constitutional convention. One consists of instituting a grass-roots, citizen endeavor, designed to acquaint as many voters as possible with the convention and involve them in some form of participatory activity, even if only by voting. The other approach seeks to achieve more limited, specific objectives through professional public relations services in a well-financed campaign. The two are neither singularly exhaustive nor mutually exclusive and may be conducted simultaneously. Both were used in preparing for Hawaii's 1968 convention, and by separate committees whose cooperation was more nominal than real. Since their objectives were not wholly identical they may be treated as complementary rather than competitive, although, on review, it is impossible not to measure the efficacy of one committee's effort against that of the other, using the common component of dollars expended for results achieved.

Publicity on the Half-shell: The 1968 Governor's Constitutional Convention Public Information Committee

The signing of the 1967 legislative measure appropriating $100,000 for pre-convention publicity immediately raised the question of how the money should be spent and who should be responsible. There was even the possibility of augmenting the state appropriation with Title I federal money and expanding the scope of the campaign. Accordingly, at the suggestion of the state budget bureau, the University of Hawaii drew up and submitted a detailed educational program to the governor, budgeted for $150,000. The university's proposal contemplated an undertaking extending over eight months, use of the mass media by way of encouraging and supplementing extensive citizen involvement, and providing a forum for candidate exposure.

The governor, however, had different plans. Since he originally was of the opinion that the convention was unnecessary, and later indicated that there were only a few major issues to be brought before the convention, he could not be expected to favor expenditure of state funds in a manner which presaged an unlimited convention reviewing the entire constitution. In view of political rivalry with the lieutenant governor, the statutory authorization to transfer the decision-making responsibility to him would remain unexercised. Everything considered, it was safest to retain control over the funds in the governor's office.

At the request of the governor, a Honolulu-based public relations consortium presented him with a generalized program for action. It called for a short period of intensive utilization of all media available in Hawaii, including newspapers, radio and television, immediately before the election of delegates. A small part of the funds would be kept in reserve for post-convention publicity. The governor then appointed a committee representing the three branches of government, as well as business, education and labor. For "executive" efficiency, its size was kept to 12, which meant that over half of its membership was comprised of public officeholders, including the governor's own administrative assistant. The Governor's Constitutional Convention Public Information Committee then approved the details and implemented the general public relations proposal previously agreed to by the governor. Although during the course of legislative consideration reference had been made to using state funds to provide exposure for candidates running as delegates, first the governor and later his committee concluded the language of the enabling legislation precluded direct candidate involvement. The committee viewed its pre-convention activities as limited to finding and publicizing the function and purpose of the constitutional convention and encouraging public participation at both voter and delegate levels. These activities would be designed to ensure public presentation of contrary views on the major issues likely to have the broadest effects on the widest segment of the public.

The public relations staff first compiled brief analyses of each article in Hawaii's constitution to provide background data for the members of the governor's committee. Using these analyses, the members were requested to identify key issues. When this proved unrewarding the staff put together a list of more than 80 possible convention issues, and, in a single session, the committee reduced them into nine workable groupings. These categories became the bases for radio and television panels, and for newspaper advertisements presenting proponent and opponent views, as well as general information about the convention and the election of delegates.

The governor's attitude toward the convention was mirrored by the committee. In the chairman's first public relations release he indicated it was the sentiment of his committee that the Hawaii state constitution was a sound document which required a minimum of change. Like the governor he referred to reapportionment and the lifting of the funded state debt limitation as specifics warranting convention attention. The initial newspaper advertisement placed by the committee reiterated the theme of excellence, and implied that it was only necessary for the voters to be informed concerning the various potential issues because the "experts" recommended extreme changes in their areas of specialization and "their cumulative expertise could result in extensive changes in the entire document."

The governor's committee was a long time in organizing and agreeing on the projected plans. The members were busy men, and with the chairman frequently absent from the state, it proved difficult to hold meetings. Actually the delay was not crucial since the original proposal was for a short and intensive program late in the campaigning. On March 30, approximately two and a half months before the election, the program got under way. The major thrust was a nine-week series of half-hour television shows, scheduled simultaneously over all Honolulu stations at a prime time early each Saturday evening. Coordinated with the series were advertisements in all major Hawaii newspapers and on a number of radio stations. The TV programs followed a panel discussion format, while the newspaper advertisements presented the arguments for and against (always equally balanced in number), with one or more issues clustered under the nine categories previously identified. The final activity of the committee was putting together a three-color, eight-page tabloid insert in both Honolulu daily newspapers, reproducing the series of advertisements and supplementing them with pictures, a complete copy of the state constitution, the names of all convention candidates and the locations of all precinct voting places.

The reaction to the committee's program was mixed. Designed to attract attention, the first newspaper advertisement started with the heading, "You paid for this, READ IT! WHY CON-CON?" and ended with the admonition, "Read these ads, your tax dollars are paying for them." Subsequent advertisements were a little less truculent in tone. The television program normally featured community leaders to sustain interest, and most likely would not have received as many viewers if competing programs had been permitted on other stations. The preemption of all TV stations for the same broadcast earned the objection of an editorial likening it to the deprivation of liberty in Big Brother fashion.

In all the committee spent a little over $90,000, returning to the state treasury $9,615 of the $100,000 appropriated. Quite probably the balance would have been used if committee plans had been followed to mount a small post-convention campaign. This proved unnecessary, as the convention arranged for such a campaign. Review of expenditures shows

EXPENDITURES OF GOVERNOR'S CONSTITUTIONAL CONVENTION
PUBLIC INFORMATION COMMITTEE

Newspaper Advertising	$27,385.00
Direct Mail*	19,292,00
Television	18,275.00
Radio	5,485.00
Production Items	9,735.00
Administration	10,213.00
	$90,385.00

* Direct mail includes approximately $16,000 for "outside printing" used as newspaper insert. The balance of this item covers mail costs, miscellaneous.

that almost half of the total was for printing charges. If the 15 percent that public relations firms receive from the mass media as commission for placing advertising is added to the "administration" item, the consortium which administered the program of the governor's committee received over 18 percent of the $90,000, not much less than the total sum spent by the Citizens' Committee on the Constitutional Convention.

Publicity on a Shoestring: The 1968
Citizens' Committee on the Constitutional Convention

Although many men very actively participated, and it was headed by a male, the Citizens' Committee on the Constitutional Convention was primarily a women's undertaking. When in mid-1967 the members of the American Association of University Women, the Junior League of Honolulu, and the League of Women Voters discovered that each organization was contemplating embarking on some form of citizen-education program for the constitutional convention, they decided to pool efforts and ask other interested organizations to join with them. What they proposed was a large-scale conference approximately six months before the election which would educate the public on constitutional issues and stimulate individuals to stand as delegates to the convention. For the first luncheon meeting 54 organizations were contacted and about 40 sent representatives. By the time the group disbanded, its membership had grown to over 250 persons, including representatives from 97 business, church, civic, fraternal, governmental, labor, political party, professional, social and other community organizations.

In addition to the highly motivated members of the three womens' organizations, the son of the 1950 convention's president served as temporary chairman of the committee. A respected judge, known for his competence in community affairs, it was only to be expected that he would be chosen for the permanent chairmanship. When the group elected its other officers at its second meeting, it was more than happenstance that a representative of the A. A. U. W. became vice chairman, another from the Junior League was designated as secretary, and, later, the representative from the League of Women Voters was appointed to the key post of public information. Supplementing these officers in comprising a "working committee" were a co-opted controller, treasurer, constitutional convention conference coordinator, and the 13 chairmen of the 12 subcommittees (the Subcommittee on Continuing Informational Effort had two co-chairmen). A small executive group, headed by the chairman, carried responsibility for most of the day-to-day decision making. Originally a policy group had been proposed with one representative from each interested organization, but, as the activities of the citizens' committee evolved, the general luncheon sessions became the "policy" body which ratified proposals brought before it.

The attention of the persons assembled at the second luncheon was called to the sign-up sheets for 12 suggested subcommittees. Later the subcommittees were urged to expand their membership beyond the number obtained at the general meetings. In all, 142 people worked on the subcommittees, with some volunteering for assignments and dropping out, their places taken by other citizens. Each committee nominally selected its own chairman. The executive group within the "working committee" designated the temporary chairman to facilitate their first meetings, however, and in most cases the same individuals became permanent chairmen of the subcommittees. The persons playing key roles in organizing the citizens' committee were careful to have both political parties represented on each committee, men and women included, and in other ways each committee so structured as to arrive at a balanced decision. When a subcommittee chairman proved inadequate for his assignments, diplomatically the executive group would suggest ways for another to assist in his stead. The relative jurisdiction of the subcommittees is indicated by their titles: Constitution and the Convention; State-

County Relationships; Tax and Finance; Judicial Article; Bill of Rights; Ethics; Legislative and Executive; Cultural Affairs; Health and Welfare; Conservation and Planning; Elections; Education; Amendment; Initiative, Referendum and Recall; and Continuing Informational Effort.

The citizens' committee developed a style of administrative decentralization which obtained maximum participation by all volunteers, while at the same time maintaining a competent coordinating group at the center to provide direction when needed and to ensure that deadlines were met. General program objectives were brought to and approved by the "policy" committee, background preparatory work was then allocated to the subcommittees, but full authority to keep everything moving and objectives achieved was assigned to the few extremely dedicated individuals placed at the strategic posts in the executive group.

Within their assigned spheres of interest, the subcommittees had the responsibility to:

1) Collect background information in a form which could be made readily available to interested persons;

2) Ascertain the proposals being seriously advanced for submission to the constitutional convention and induce their phrasing in precise language suitable for adoption;

3) Encourage discussion of all proposals and provide coordination, material, speakers and advice in aid of discussion programs;

4) Answer all bona fide public requests for information;

5) Act as a resource of personnel and information for the secretariat and the Subcommittee on Continuing Informational Effort;

6) Develop and recommend programs designed to sharpen issues, increase citizen interest and educate the public; and

7) Select and present the material to be covered at the constitutional conference sponsored by the citizens' committee.

Each subcommittee was requested to work out a program for public presentation within its respective area, with radio, television and press used for this purpose. Specifically, it was asked to prepare drafts for one-minute "spots" for radio and television, highlighting the issues which would come before the convention. Also, it furnished short- to medium-length articles suitable for press release concentrating on the pro and con aspects of each issue. Lists of names of people "whose opinions are valued in the community" and who would be willing to record announcements for radio and television use were prepared. Advance press releases and fact sheets about speaking engagements arranged by the subcommittees were channelled to central public relations, as was advance information about any publications prepared by the subcommittees. Maximum public impact was obtained through the central public relations office.

The activity of each chairman was crucial to his subcommittee's success. Examples such as the following abound of the low-keyed but firm direction contributed by the successful chairman, while maintaining full committee involvement and inviting the cooperation of every individual within the committee:

> The Bill of Rights subcommittee will meet. . . .
>
> This meeting has been called to allow each and every subcommittee member to review and approve the January 25th [Constitutional Convention Conference] program and to meet the panel members.
>
> You are urged to bring to this meeting any provocative questions or statements pertaining to the Bill of Rights, private or civil, especially those relating to the State of Hawaii or any other material pertinent to the program.
>
> Example: public funds should, if needed, be used for private or sectarian school bus transportation. . . .
>
> After a format is decided upon, this material will be printed in some convenient form to be used as handout leaflets. Do you know how we can get 1,000 or more leaflets printed free or at cost?
>
> All people attending the conference . . . should receive a copy even if they cannot attend the Bill of Rights sessions.
>
> Please check with your respective organizations, clubs, unions, etc. encouraging them to submit resolutions or proposals for our January 25th Constitutional Convention Conference. Maybe you or someone you know would like to submit a resolution or proposal for the conference. Please feel free to do so. All ideas are encouraged.
>
> See you Tuesday. . . .

While the original objective of bringing the various community organizations together was to hold a conference for the constitutional convention, it was the consensus of the representatives attending the early organizational meetings that the committee's purpose should be focused more toward citizen education en toto, than singularly on the conference. As a result the activities of the citizens' committee may be divided into two stages, the first directed toward planning and then running a major conference, and the second a continuing educational effort initially conceived to last until the revised constitution was presented to the voters for their approval. Later this was shortened to conclude with the convening of the constitutional convention.

At the time the citizens' committee was being formed, the University of Hawaii was presenting its proposal for a constitutional convention education program to the governor. If its bid proved successful, the committee would supplement the university's activities, so that their efforts could be dovetailed and the university approached for financial assistance. When this did not materialize, it became obvious that the bulk if not all of the money required would have to be raised by the citizens' committee's own efforts.

By the third meeting of the committee, approximately a month after it got under way, subcommittees had been organized, a suggested planning time schedule circulated for the projected conference, a conference headquarters established with its telephone manned by volunteers, and donations were being collected. The groundwork for an extensive public relations program had been laid by enlisting the cooperation of professional personnel from public relations firms and the press, radio and television. Later many were to provide assistance in the form of arranging programs, laying out copy, preparing materials on the production facilities of some stations and duplicating them for broadcast on others, and in other ways furnishing the necessary expertise and technical services.

One of the early decisions which proved important to the success of the constitutional convention conference was the selection of a program chairman charged with overall responsibility for the three-day conference. Assisted by others in the working committee, and particularly the members of the inner executive group, he received program segments from the various subcommittees and fitted together a cohesive program designed to attract a wide gamut of persons interested for a variety of reasons in the forthcoming constitutional convention. The ability of the conference coordinator was so well demonstrated by his performance in organizing the conference that six months later, when chairmen were designated for the standing committees of the convention, as an elected delegate he was named to chair the key Committee on Legislative Apportionment and Districting.

The citizens' committee worked with the conference center of the University of Hawaii in making the technical preparations for the constitutional convention. Conference center personnel aided in planning, laying out promotional material, and, later, setting up the physical facilities at one of the large convention hotels in Waikiki. The program remained the responsibility of the citizens' committee.

To provide content as well as glamor to the conference, and to spread the limited resources of the citizens' committee, arrangements were made for five distinguished mainland commentators to participate in the three-day conference, with their costs underwritten separately by the American Judicature Society, the Council of State Governments, the Hawaii State Foundation on Culture and the Arts, the National and Hawaii American Civil Liberties Union, and the National Municipal League. They served primarily as feature speakers at conference luncheons. Carrying the brunt of the program were over a hundred academic, community and political leaders who discussed the pros and cons of the major issues likely to come before the constitutional convention, usually through the device of panel presentations. Heading this group, and addressing the opening session of the conference, was Governor John A. Burns, who reiterated that Hawaii's constitution was basically sound and that a full-scale constitutional convention was unnecessary.

As part of the preparatory work for the conference, some ten thousand promotional brochures were mailed. The subjects to be covered each day were listed and recipients requested to indicate the days on which they desired to attend. Costs, including registration fee and lunch, were $6.00 for one day, $11.00 for two, and $15.00 for the entire conference. The newspapers and other media provided excellent advance publicity and, on the opening day, when Governor Burns spoke he had a "standing room only" audience estimated to number 500. In all, some 711 persons attended the three-day conference, 676 paying $7,047 in registration fees. What was anticipated to be a money-losing operation, the deficit to be met by soliciting contributions, to the surprise of everyone turned in a profit of $1,200. Included among the panel discussants and the audience were many of the candidates, announced and unannounced, later to run for the constitutional convention. The conference admirably served the dual purpose of directing the attention of the public to the forthcoming election and convention, and also helped to clarify the nature of the issues.

One of the unexpected results of the conference was the organizing of comparable activity on the Neighbor Islands. The citizens' committee was Honolulu staffed and its efforts primarily aimed at the bulk of the state's population resident on the island of Oahu. A group paralleling the committee was formed in the county of Hawaii, and it ran a two-day, countywide conference on convention issues. Later in May, a Kauai citizens' committee sponsored a day-long conference on that island. A great degree of widespread citizen participation was achieved on the islands by their committees.

With the successful completion of its three-day conference, the citizens' committee on Oahu directed its attention to other activities. The committee's public relations chief produced a weekly "Con Commentary" radio call-in program. The committee prepared and mailed folders to church, community and service organizations listing both issues and sources of information. Included were references to constitutional convention series carried on both educational and commercial television stations, the latter produced by the governor's committee, many of whose panel participants had been suggested by the citizens' committee. Mention was also made of the University of Hawaii's Lyceum and Speakers Bureau which met requests from organizations for speakers, frequently persons recruited by the citizens' committee. Also included in the brochure was reference to the Library of Hawaii's collection of convention materials maintained at all branches throughout the state, and to the eight-week seminars on constitutional convention issues conducted as extension courses under university auspices. The Subcommittee on Continuing Informational Effort had arranged for the printing of 50,000 copies of Hawaii's state constitution, and this continued to be distributed by the state libraries throughout the entire period prior to the convention. The libraries, in coordination with the committee, also prepared literature on events related to the constitutional convention.

One of the subcommittees whose work expanded after the conclusion of the constitutional convention conference was the Subcommittee on Continuing Informational Effort, which gathered basic biographical information by questionnaires sent to all candidates. This was supplemented by searches of other sources when replies were not forthcoming. All of this data was printed in a 16 half-page roster of candidates, with photographs, published as a talbloid insert in a joint Sunday issue of the *Honolulu Star-Bulletin* and *Advertiser*. What many readers probably ignored was that the usual short items newspapers use to fill out the columns were for this particular section replaced with short fillers supplied by the committee pertinent to voting for candidates, holding the convention, and obtaining information on issues. In all the citizens' committee succeeded in publishing brief biographies of 360 of the 378 announced candidates, providing background information on the many unknown individuals who were running for public office for the first time.

The final activity of the citizens' committee was a three-day symposium at the University of Hawaii, held after the delegates were elected. Delegates-elect had previously been asked by mail to identify their areas of interest and, to the extent possible, the program was arranged to comply. Seventy-five delegates attended the symposium; of the seven who were not present three were known to be on the mainland. Each delegate received an information kit containing National Municipal League constitutional studies, copies of recent constitutions and convention rules, and other mainland and locally produced materials.

The symposium featured four mainland specialists on constitutional revision. In addition, delegates had an opportunity to consult with local government officials who shortly would be called on to provide services to the convention. The committee also arranged for the delegates to meet with the attorneys who had appeared to argue Hawaii's apportionment case before the U. S. Supreme Court.

A good part of the symposium was devoted to sessions on the experiences of other conventions, and the extent to which they were transferable to Hawaii. The four-man team from the mainland had only been minimally briefed on some of the quirks of Hawaiian politics, which resulted in their offhandedly expressing some opinions which ran contrary to past political practices as well as the positions publicly taken by delegates. All of this was received without rancor, and the symposium as a whole was judged by the participants as very successful. Privately the legislator-delegates indicated that much which was covered would be already known to legislators or persons active in the political arena. They welcomed the symposium, however, as the same information communicated by an unbiased group would be more acceptable to the independent delegates than if it had come from the legislators. As a consequence they treated the symposium as of material value in helping to overcome the suspicion of the political newcomers. Although not publicized, one of the major reasons for the citizens' committee sponsoring the symposium was to enable the delegates to become familiar with each other. Watching the little clusters of delegates group and regroup during the three-day symposium, and legislators mix with the non-politically oriented and deliberately allow independents to take a predominent role in raising questions was visual proof of the success of this objective. When the symposium ended at noon of the third day, and the delegates later reassembled elsewhere for their first formal caucus, they were now personally acquainted and ready to turn to the business of organizing the convention.

After the symposium the citizens' committee faced the question of whether to continue in existence during the convention, and, possibly, then help "sell" the proposed amendments in the post-convention period. The members of the small executive committee recognized that as an organization the citizens' committee had no agreed position and, in fact, it had deliberately sought to enlist the participation of individuals with conflicting points of view. It would be difficult, if not impossible, for the committee to reach a consensus on any issue, and to lobby for it before the convention or support it in the post-convention period. Funds were about exhausted; the major purpose of the committee had been accomplished; it was time to disband. The $485.80 remaining in the committee's treasury was formally transferred to the Library of Hawaii to aid its continuing educational effort.

The citizens' committee operated on a total budget of $20,000, not counting the thousands of dollars worth of free services donated by individuals and organizations. Of the money used only $1,500 came from the $100,000 appropriated by the legislature for pre-convention education, and this after the election of delegates. When the committee found that it did not have enough funds to sponsor the final symposium, it requested $1,350 from the governor's committee to cover the cost of published materials to be distributed to the delegates and $150 for miscellaneous symposium expenses. The balance of the money consisted of contributions from individuals and organizations within Hawaii, net receipts of the three-day conference, and a donation from a mainland foundation. The

CITIZENS' COMMITTEE RECEIPTS

Misc. contributions	
individual and organization	$ 3,221
Constitutional Conference	
registration fees[a]	7,047
Sears-Roebuck Foundation[b]	5,000
Governor's Committee[c]	1,500
	$16,768
Printing constitution[d]	3,200
(7 local firms)	
	$19,968

[a] Expenditures of conference $5,839.
[b] Used for printing Candidates' Tabloid.
[c] Materials for Delegate Symposium.
[d] Expended separately for printing state constitution.

bulk of expenditures went for printing, $11,000 alone for duplicating the state constitution and publishing the Candidates' Tabloid prior to the election. Nearly $6,000 was for the costs of the constitutional convention conference. The balance covered a miscellany of items.

Governor's Committee and Citizens' Committee Relationships

What of the citizens' committee's relations with the governor's committee? The former had held three well-publicized organizational meetings before the governor named his own committee. When he did so, and failed to include anyone from the citizens' committee, it appeared to many that this was a deliberate repudiation of the citizen effort. Later the governor indicated that he expected there would be close coordination of the groups' efforts, but resisted the suggestion that, to achieve liaison and avoid needless overlapping and duplication, he name representatives from the citizens' group to his committee. To the politically suspicious it seemed as if the governor was intent on assuring that any pre-convention "tooling up" with state funds would be conducted in the manner he approved.

Two days before the opening of the constitutional convention conference the chairman of the governor's committee issued a publicity release in which he endorsed the activities of the citizens' committee. The chairman, the governor and several members of his committee took part in the conference as program speakers. Meanwhile the plans of the governor's committee remained confidential.

In February the citizens' committee requested that formal relationships be established between the two groups. Since the governor's committee was reportedly not considering activating any program prior to the middle of February, the citizens' committee had been able to receive public service time and space from the communications media and substantial private donations from individuals and organizations for printing materials. Solicitation for such assistance after that date was hampered by the failure of the governor's committee to announce the purposes for which it proposed to spend state funds. Finally, over a month later, the governor's committee "came out of seclusion" and announced the general format of its program to publicize the issues likely to arise at the state constitutional convention. It was explained that committee members felt that they had to clarify their own position before having participation from the citizens' committee.

The top officials of the citizens' group were invited to the public meeting where the plans of the governor's committee were revealed. As commented on by a newspaper reporter, "The first half hour was more or less a public fumbling for amicability, which included a number of public statements for the press, interposed with long, awkward silences. Both committees then went into a 20-minute, closed-door session to establish a working relationship. Afterward, members of the Citizens' Committee accompanied the staff of the Governor's Committee to receive a copy of its program plans."

Actually, there proved to be little need for coordinating organization. The governor's committee focused narrowly on publicizing issues, and that impersonally through the mass media. The activities of the citizens' committee were broader and people-centered, and its plans to publish candidates' biographical sketches and work with the delegates-elect in no way overlapped the efforts of the governor's committee. When, in a brochure listing sources of information on constitutional issues, the citizens' committee included the television series schedule of the governor's committee, it was regarded as an attempt to demonstrate the fact that the two groups were now cooperating. Perhaps the best proof that they saw their objectives as complementary if not fully shared was the $1,500 contribution by the governor's committee to help defray the cost of the symposium for delegates undertaken by the other group.

The program of the governor's committee was conceived and implemented by public relations experts, and was undertaken with professional flair and the expenditure of a correspondingly large amount of money. The citizens' committee aimed for the broadest possible participation, sometimes was amateurish, but succeeded in enlisting the voluntary assistance of the broad swath of the mass media and achieving a wide range of goals despite its limited funds. A day after the citizens' committee published its Candidates' Tabloid, the governor's committee produced its supplement for insertion in each of Honolulu's daily newspapers. As a commentator at the time acidly remarked on the differences between the two publications, and, impliedly, between the committees:

> Contrast the paid advertising supplements last week of the two organizations. The Governor's Committee supplement, in color, was very attractive but contained nothing new. The Citizens' Committee, on the other hand, was able to produce a supplement which was truly helpful, for it contained the biographies of 360 of the 378 announced candidates. True, the supplement was not very attractive, but it was extremely useful and cost the taxpayers nothing.
>
> The performance of the two agencies should be a good reminder to all of us that whenever we let the government do things for us which we can do better for ourselves, it not only costs the taxpayer money, but the job can be inferior (*Honolulu Star-Bulletin*, June 2, 1968).

4.

The Elections

For the 1950 and 1968 constitutional conventions, the major problems faced in the administration of the elections for delegates were encountered in the preliminary decisions necessary to get their operations under way. It was decided early that nonpartisan special elections would be most fitting to the character of a constitutional convention. The primary and runoff final election of the 1950 convention were also advocated for the 1968 body but, in the final legislative compromise, a single election prevailed. Once such basic matters were resolved, for the most part the holding of the special elections merely required the adaptation of the established procedures for registration, nomination, balloting and canvassing to meeting the specifics of choosing convention delegates. The one exception arose out of Hawaii's shifting to computer-counted balloting, so that the special election in 1968 introduced the voters to the use of punch-card ballots. Extra money and effort had to be expended by the state in training election officials and familiarizing the voters with the use of the new ballot, and because of this the $295,000 estimated cost of the 1968 convention election exceeded that of any previous primary or general election in Hawaii.

Voter Registration and Turnout

Candidates met the same qualifications as those required to register as a voter—minimum age of 21 in 1950, 20 in 1968; residence of a year;

and literacy in English or Hawaiian. An amendment to the Organic Act permitted territorial legislators to run in 1950 without violating the stricture against dual officeholding, and the state constitution later continued the same waiver in more general language. Official nomination papers were filed for each candidate, signed by 15 (25 in 1950) or more registered voters of the district in which the candidate planned to run, accompanied by a fee of $25. Neither nomination papers nor election ballots carried any designation of political party affiliation.

From the start it was apparent that voter interest and participation in the 1968 election were going to be poorer than in 1950. Considerably fewer people registered to vote for the 1968 special election (242,627) than at the immediately preceding 1966 state primary and general elections. In contrast, registration for the constitutional convention primary in 1950 proved to be the highest primary registration in the territory's history (although a little lower than the registration for the 1948 general election). Later, voter turnout figures showed a corresponding difference in the attitudes of the Islanders toward the significance of the conventions. At the primary and, later, the final runoff elections in 1950, 73 and 79 percent, respectively, of the registered voters went to the polls. In 1968 only 45 percent cast ballots for delegates and, in the city and county of Honolulu, where the bulk of the voters live, the percentage dipped down to a low 39. It was only because of the nearly two-thirds turnout of the Neighbor Island vote, contributed to by interest in the charter ratifications also taking place on Kauai and Hawaii, that the state's performance at the special election did not compare even more unfavorably with that of the territorial convention vote.

The failure of Hawaii's voters to go to the polls in 1968 can hardly be blamed on the candidates' failure to electioneer. Nor can it be attributed to any lack of effort on the part of the mass media to keep the public informed about the candidates and their campaigning, and to seek to stimulate popular interest concerning issues which the convention might be called on to consider. There was just not enough drama surrounding the special election to make it interesting to the average citizen. Neither the candidates nor the issues was exciting, there was no clash of competing parties, and the voters stayed home. In 1950 the political parties participated more actively in the campaigning, and, above partisanship, the overriding cause of statehood brought the voters out. Of the 18 candidates who won outright election in the 1950 primary, all but one were staunch statehood supporters.

The Candidates

Once arrangements were concluded for holding the elections, it became open season for the newspapers to muse publicly over the identity of potential candidates, much to the surprise of some citizens who had not contemplated running for delegate until they saw their names linked with the convention. Later the public press decried the slowness of announced candidates to file their nomination papers, meanwhile keeping public count of those officially in the race. As the deadline for filing approached, with the field of candidates still small, the tone of the newspaper comment grew more strident. Each day's new entrants received prominent mention. And when the deadline neared, the same phenomena occurred both in 1950 and 1968. During the last few days the tempo of filing sharply increased as candidates who were waiting to gauge the field decided they stood a chance to win. With the last nomination paper filed, it was found that all delegates' seats would be contested, most many times over. Relative to the positions to be filled, more candidates (378 total) filed in each of the counties in 1968 than they did 18 years earlier (243). The differences in ratios are not striking and the explanation is undoubtedly complex. With little popular interest, and no political party involvement evidenced, opportunity was presented for the "has-been" to attempt a political comeback and for the newcomer to test his voting strength. Unquestionably, also, the mass media's call for public-spirited citizens to serve in the conventions attracted many political unknowns into a venture for which they were poorly prepared and had little chance of success.

RATIO OF CANDIDATES TO DELEGATE POSTS TO BE FILLED

	1950 (63)	*1968 (82)*
Hawaii	3 1/12	3 2/9
Maui	2 5/9	2 5/6
Kauai	2 2/3	3 1/4
N. Islands	2 3/4	3
Oahu "4th"	5 4/9	5 1/3
Oahu "5th"	3 5/6	4 4/5
Oahu	4 2/3	5
Average	3 7/8	4 3/5

In 1950, 243 candidates; in 1968, 378 candidates.

As was to be expected, the multiple-delegate district races drew more candidates than those contests in which a single delegate was to be chosen. Sheer statistical averages of success apparently did not materially influence the candidates, and in 1968 the larger the number of delegates to be elected for the at-large, multi-delegate districts, the greater the disproportion of candidates who filed, and the lower their relative chances of success.

CANDIDATES FILING FOR MULTI-DELEGATE DISTRICTS, 1968 CONVENTION

Posts in Multi-Delegate Districts	Number of Candidates Filing	Ratio
2-delegate districts (2)	4/5	(2 1/4)
3-delegate districts (5)	7/10/10/12/13	(2 7/15)
4-delegate districts (1)	25	(6 1/4)
5-delegate districts (2)	21/32	(5 3/10)
6-delegate districts (1)	36	(6)

Both in 1950 and in 1968 there were relatively more aspirants for delegate posts on Oahu than in the Neighbor Islands. Most likely, variations in urbanization and all that it connotes bears relation to this differential, as is indicated by the area formerly included in the old, more rural "5th district" on Oahu attracting fewer candidates per delegate post than did the highly urbanized area within Honolulu. But other factors must also have contributed, as is suggested by the fact that in the Neighbor Islands a non-Hawaii born candidate had little chance of success at the polls.

Campaigning in 1950 was more organized, and rallies probably received greater voter attendance than at the recent constitutional convention election, this even though the newspapers of 1950 carried repeated plaints of the poor show of interest. The secretary of the territory arranged for nonpartisan rallies at which all candidates appeared. The two minutes allotted each speaker prior to the primary, and five minutes prior to the final election, allowed little time to develop issues and, cumulatively, made for a dull rally. It was found that attendance increased after musical entertainment was added. This was just at the end of the era of old-style, unsophisticated, Hawaiian politiking, when personality politics held sway, and a voter went to a political rally to be entertained and possibly fed. Radio and newspaper advertisements might be used, and tons of printed literature distributed by doorbell ringers, but the community rally still remained the focus around which candidate-voter contact turned.

The Political Parties

Despite the official nonpartisan character of the elections, in 1950 Republicans and Democrats took an aggressive interest in electing delegates of their respective parties. Political leaders openly asserted that they were working to elect a majority of their party to the convention. The Republican party, particularly, was extremely active at the precinct level, organizing meetings and holding political rallies to which only Republican candidates were invited. The campaigns of other community groups to support convention candidates who were members of their organizations also led to criticisms that the nonpartisanship theme of the campaign was being violated. This reached the point where the secretary of the territory, while serving as acting governor, publicly condemned the growing party involvement and urged greater bipartisanship. When the Honolulu Junior Chamber of Commerce painted markers on the sidewalks, distributed handbills, placed spot radio announcements, and had slides shown in the theatres reminding voters to go to the polls, they were communicating with an audience which had already been prepared for involvement.

In 1968 political party participation was muted at best and, except for personal organizations within a legislator's own district, for the most part was non-existent. Candidates conducted individualistic campaigns, depending on door-to-door contact, TV appearances, radio and newspaper advertisements, bumper stickers, signs kept within the limited size permitted by law, and handbill distribution. Some ran polls on issues and printed the results, including their own stands. One candidate bought a whole page in both of Honolulu's daily newspapers and covered it with a 7,000-word statement. Efforts at mounting rallies at which all candidates from a district could appear mostly proved ineffective. Twenty-thousand leaflets distributed in one area on Oahu resulted in the attendance of a crowd of 200. More frequently, candidates outnumbered audiences at meetings. While the citizens' committee and the governor's committee each in its own way sought to acquaint the voters with the major issues, and through this encourage them to make a choice among candidates, the transference had limited success. The candidates tended to raise issues in their campaigns, and then shift to others as they sensed a lack of voter interest; few expressed commitment in any major area. When the 378 candidates were polled on issues for the convention, only

96 designated apportionment, 61 voting age, and 51 judiciary reform, this despite reapportionment being the cause for calling the convention. Half of the candidates named no issue at all! The most controversial issue, perhaps it should be called a "non-issue," was whether legislators should run as delegates, and it was to this that the defeat of a few incumbents can be traced.

In 1950, beside covert party endorsement, a few slates of candidates were circulated, some announced, most anonymous. Slate making was more actively practiced in 1968, and three of the Islands' potent unions (AFL-CIO, ILWU and the United Public Workers) each publicly endorsed sufficient candidates to constitute a majority of the convention. The effect of slate making proved inconclusive in 1950, with each group having some of its endorsed candidates elected. In 1968 the same occurred, but was accompanied with the defeat of some candidates who appeared on all three union slates and the election of others who had failed to receive a single labor endorsement. Such influence as the unions could claim in channeling the vote—winning candidates comprising from a little under 50 percent to 70 percent of the slates—needs to be discounted by the fact that incumbent legislators comprised over two-thirds of each slate's successful candidates. By way of explaining why more of their endorsees did not win, union leaders could point to the low turnout of voters and note that this traditionally boded ill for unions due to the larger than normal component of middle class and smaller proportion of workingmen who went to the polls.

Technical inadequacies in polling may also have contributed to the defeat of some candidates in 1968. In four of the contests with long lists of candidates it was necessary to print their names on both the front and back of the computer-card ballot. Disregarding the admonition carried on the ballot to "vote both sides," some voters failed to turn their ballots over when choosing among the candidates. In these four races, 17 of the 20 winning candidates' names were printed on the front of the ballot. The lack of familiarity with the new system of voting was epitomized by one cautious citizen who not only punched out the holes on the ballot which he wanted voted, but also covered the balance with tape to assure they could not enter into the tally.

Among the field of candidates the voters in 1968 had a slightly larger number of women. Data for many of the occupational categories is not available for the 1950 primary election. Those provided for the 18 candidates who won outright, and the 90 who were nominated at the primary and then stood for the runoff final election five weeks later, reveals that "businessmen," of all categories when grouped together, did relatively better in 1968 than in 1950. On the other hand a very small number of professors and teachers ran in 1950 and only two university students had the temerity to seek election. Unlike the experience in 1950 when two out of three professors were elected, in 1968 the voters gave short shrift to a much larger group of university faculty. University students who filed in considerable numbers (compared to 1950) suffered the same fate as their professors. Teachers at other levels fared better. There is little question but that public disapproval of student disturbances on the University of Hawaii campus and, particularly, the acrimony engendered over the question of granting tenure to a controversial professor, helps explain the defeat of university-identified personnel. In 1950 and 1968, incumbent legislators constituted only a small proportion of the total candidate field but enjoyed a much greater than average success.

CANDIDATES AND DELEGATES COMPARED

	1950 Elections			1968 Elections	
	Filed (% of candidates)	Won at Primary (% of primary candidates)	Won at Final (% of delegates)	Filed (% of candidates)	Won (% of delegates)
Women	23 (9%)	7 (6%)	5 (8%)	54 (14%)	8 (10%)
All "Businessmen" . . [a]		43 (40%)	25 (40%)	123[b] (33%)	35 (43%)
Lawyers . . [a]		26 (24%)	19 (30%)	62[c] (16%)	25[c] (30%)
Doctors, etc. . . [a]		7 (6%)	5 (8%)	8 (2%)	2 (2%)
Teachers . . [a]		8 (7%)	5 (8%)	36[d] (10%)	5 (6%)
Professors	3[e] (1%)	3[e] (3%)	2[e] (3%)	15 (4%)	1 (1%)
Students . . [a]		2 (2%)	. . [f]	17[g] (4%)	1 (1%)
Incumb. Legis.	22 (9%)	17 (16%)	12 (19%)	45 (12%)	37 (45%)

[a] Unavailable.

[b] Note that occupations of 27 candidates (of total 378) unknown.

[c] For candidates, include judges, government employed attorneys, district court practitioners; does not include four with law degrees, but who have not taken bar examination, not practicing, etc.; for delegates, does not include one with law degree, etc.

[d] Includes educational administrators, and seven retired teachers apparently not otherwise employed.

[e] Includes one retired professor serving as U. H. regent.

[f] One student subsequently appointed as delegate to fill a vacancy.

[g] Full time, or approximately full time. One delegate who subsequently returned to U. H. as a student, listed as "businessman" at time of election.

A large percentage of the candidates at the 1950 elections had never before sought office, nor had they been actively identified in any way with partisan party politics. The same was true for the 1968 convention election, where nearly 70 percent of the candidates who filed reported they were political neophytes. On balance it is doubtful that they fared much better in 1950 than in the more recent convention election, even though a larger number of incumbent officers contested and won delegate seats in 1968.

Election to the 1950 convention furnished no appreciable advantage to the candidates in 1968. About as many lost (five) as were successful (seven), not including among the latter a 1950 delegate who had resigned from that convention at the outset because of prior Communist party association.

The 1968 election returns demonstrated that the large influx of people into Hawaii since statehood had not tarnished the political attractiveness of the *kamaaina*. In none of the 19 contests in the Neighbor Islands was a non-Hawaii born candidate elected. (In 11 cases, and probably 13, Island-born triumphed over persons born outside of Hawaii; in the remaining, only Island-born candidates contested.) On Oahu, 13 delegates born outside of Hawaii were elected, this out of a total of 63 delegates from the island. In addition, recent arrivals who ran for office were ill-advised, as a majority of the successful non-local delegates (seven) could point to long-term residence of over 20 years in Hawaii, while only four reported Hawaiian residence of five years or less.

This tendency toward parochialism is borne out further when reference is made to the delegates' island of origin. At least 15 of the 19 delegates

PLACE OF BIRTH/RESIDENCE OF CANDIDATES, 1968

	Candidates	Delegates
Island born:	209 (55%)[a]	69 (84%)[b]
Others (length of residence):		
over 20	47 (12%)	7 (9%)
11 to 20	26 (7%)	. .
6 to 10	30 (8%)	2 (2%)
5 or less	33 (9%)	4 (5%)
Unknown:	33 (9%)	. .
	378 (100%)	82 (100%)

[a] Percentage of total candidates.
[b] Percentage of delegates elected.

elected from the Neighbor Islands and 35 of the 50 Island-born delegates from Oahu hailed from the same island from which the voters elected them. For constitution drafting, Hawaii's voters preferred *kamaainas* (local born), and among them, those born on the island which they were to represent in the convention.

The large group of candidates whose age is unknown precludes close comparison of the 1968 field with the delegates elected to sit in the 1968 convention. Most bunched within the 31-50 age bracket, with the extremes of youth and senior citizen status underrepresented. The median delegate age in 1968 was 42.

1968 CONVENTION (AGES)

Ages	Candidates	Delegates
20-25	24[a]	3[b]
26-30	34	4
31-50	179	55
50+	78	18[c]
Unknown	63	2
	378	82

[a] In 1950, youngest candidate 22 years of age.
[b] In 1968, youngest delegate 20 years of age.
[c] Oldest delegate 73 in 1950, 63 in 1968.

Composition of the Conventions

Responding to newspaper encouragement that the 1950 convention should not be composed predominantly of lawyers, but "should be a good cross section of the people of Hawaii" with "both the ablest minds and the deepest devotions" (*Honolulu Advertiser,* January 11, 1950), many candidates of diverse backgrounds and good will, but little political experience, filed their nomination papers. With the elections over, the convention contained a large component of lawyers and disclosed greater evidence of mirroring the "politic" portion of the body politic than a full cross section of Hawaii's people. The same generalization holds true for the convention in 1968.

Only a negligible number of the 1950 delegates returned to sit in the 1968 convention, and the 30 percent increase in size of the latter presumably offered greater opportunity for diversity. Notwithstanding this,

DELEGATE COMPOSITION OF TWO CONVENTIONS

	1950		1968	
Occupation:				
Lawyers[a]	30%	(19)	30%	(25)
Business	40%		43%	
—sugar & pine. officers	14%	(9)	4%	(3)
—business owners	10%	(6)	9%	(7)
—other activity	16%	(10)	30%	(25)
Educators[b]	11%	(7)	7%	(6)
Doctors, Dentists,				
Optometrists	8%	(5)	2%	(2)
Housewives	5%	(3)	2%	(2)
Union Organizers	3%	(2)	2%	(2)
Full-time Public Officer	2%	(1)	2%	(2)
Retired	2%	(1)	2%	(2)
Student[c]	..		1%	(1)
Civil Service Employees	..		6%	(5)
	100%	(63)	100%*	(82)
Hawaii-born	78%	(49)	84%	(69)
Females	8%	(5)	10%	(8)
Education:				
Graduate Degree	41%	(26)	48%	(39)
Bachelor Degree	32%	(20)	21%	(17)
High School Degree[d]	16%	(10)	30%	(25)
Less or Unknown	11%	(7)	1%	(1)
	100%	(63)	100%	(82)
Ethnicity:				
Caucasian[e]	43%	(27)	27%	(22)
Chinese	8%	(5)	9%	(7)
Filipino	..		5%	(4)
Hawaiian[f]	19%	(12)	10%	(8)
Japanese	30%	(19)	46%	(38)
Korean	..		4%	(3)
	100%	(63)	100%*	(82)
Political Affiliation				
Democrat	32%	(20)[g]	68%	(45)+(11)[g]
Republican	48%	(30)	28%	(17)+(6)
Indep./Unknown	21%	(13)	4%	(3)
	100%*	(63)	100%	(82)

* Does not add up to 100% due to rounding.

[a] "Lawyers" includes district court practitioners, judges, etc.; for 1968, one delegate yet to pass his bar examination not included.

[b] In 1950, includes one educator holding full-time, administrative post (not shown under "full-time public officer").

the composition of the two delegate bodies remained remarkably similar. In the main the variances between the two reflect the shift in the base of political influence which had occurred in the Islands during the intervening 18 years. This had certain occupational and ethnic overtones and, of course, a reversal in political party control, which is all tidily demonstrated in a comparison of the delegates chosen to sit in the two conventions.

Island-born delegates still continued numerically to have the greatest share in constitution drafting, and females very little. Much the same proportion of delegates brought academic training measured by college degrees to the work of the convention and exactly the same percentage of lawyers participated. On both occasions businessmen comprised about 40 percent of the total, and educators constituted the third largest numerical grouping. Although public employees were not precluded from taking part in the 1950 convention, their participation was limited to electioneering for others. By 1968 the importance of their role in the Island polity was evinced by the five civil servants elected as delegates.

Reference to the political party affiliations of delegates reveals the peaceful revolution which had occurred in Hawaii. The majority position which the Republicans enjoyed in the 1950 convention was now surrendered to the Democrats. The delegates listed as pledged members of the Democratic party and those who voted in the 1968 Democratic primary shortly after the adjournment of the constitutional convention (and consequently are registered in the electoral rolls as Democrats) to-

---

c A university student runner-up in 1950 replaced a delegate who resigned.

d Includes some with vocational school, business school, etc., training beyond high school; in 1950 includes one with some college work, in 1968 includes nine.

e "Caucasian" includes both "Haole" and "Portuguese" which were, respectively, 23 and four in 1950 and 18 and four in 1968. The 1950 composition compared with the native born and naturalized, foreign born population in Hawaii 1950, 21 years of age and over—Caucasian, 26 percent; Chinese, 7 percent; Hawaiian, 12 percent; Japanese, 37 percent; Filipino, 13 percent; others, 4 percent.

f "Hawaiian" includes part-Hawaiians.

g For 1950, the estimates vary slightly, depending on source. For 1968, first figure provides party membership, second figure party registration at 1968 primary for persons not listed by parties and whose status otherwise unknown.

Source: Newspapers and personal inquiries; also for 1968, questionnaires completed by delegates, political party records, primary election rolls.

gether account for 68 percent of all delegates. This contrasts with 28 percent for all delegates similarly identified with the Republicans. Along with this party shift, the role allotted managerial officers of the sugar and pineapple industries was curtailed (14 percent to 4 percent), and the officers and employees of a broader swath of economic activity found theirs nearly doubled (16 percent to 30 percent). Fewer leading pillars of society, persons of acclaimed community standing, appeared in the 1968 convention. The change in the ethnic composition of the convention also was tied to this reversal of political dominance, with a reduction in the number of Caucasian and Hawaiian delegates and a corresponding jump in the Oriental component. The means for this can be traced to the election success of incumbent legislators, which helped bring into the 1968 convention the same ethnic-skewed party distribution which characterized recent Hawaii legislatures.

At the 1950 elections a brief flurry had occurred over the challenge issued by the Maui County Democratic Committee which voted to withhold its support of any territorial legislator who became a candidate for election to the convention. Former Senator Rice of Maui and the Democratic Committee noted a conflict of interest, for the convention's draft constitution had to be passed on by the territorial legislature, which morally precluded legislators' reviewing their own handiwork. Perhaps because of this, relatively fewer legislators filed, and a noticeably small proportion was successful at the polls.

Legislators as Delegates

The outcry over incumbent legislators serving as delegates in 1950 was only a whisper compared with the protests voiced at the 1968 elections. Initially it seemed as if the legislators were attempting to apportion the convention districts to their own advantage by making them coterminous with legislative districts. Later, when smaller, grouped-precinct districts were also incorporated, some of the incumbent legislators ignored the rationale for their creation (aid to non-politico), and filed candidacy from them. Given the saliency of an incumbent legislator, it appeared almost impossible for a political novice to defeat him, and, as a matter of second choice, many non-politicos filed for the at-large elections. Proportionately, not only did a larger number of legislators run in 1968, but, thanks to the convenient distribution of delegate posts which allowed incumbent legislators to space their candidacy, there was also not a single contest between incumbents.

The legislator-candidate found himself in the embarrassing position of being accused of violating the rules of fair play when he took to the hustings and campaigned, while facing the risk of defeat if he did not answer the charges of behaving improperly. Seventeen of the 45 incumbent legislator-candidates filed from grouped-precinct districts, and 15 of them were on Oahu. The fact that there were also 18 incumbents who were running in at-large races on Oahu, rather than balancing the unfavorable publicity, only fed the generalized sentiment that there were too many legislator-candidates. In seven of the state's at-large races in which legislators were candidates, only one delegate was to be elected. With 24 incumbent legislators thus standing from single-delegate districts, the impression easily spread that all legislators were taking an unfair

LEGISLATORS AS DELEGATES

	1950 (63)		1968 (82)	
Incumbent Legislators:				
Ran for Office[a]	22		45	
(as % of legislature)		(49%)		(59%)
(as % of candidates)		(9%)		(12%)
Elected	12		37	
(as % of delegates)		(19%)		(45%)
Previous Legislative Experience:				
Ran for Office[b]		. .	12[c]	
Elected	6[d]		5[e]	
(as % of delegates)		(10%)		(6%)
All Delegates with Legislative Exper.:				
Total	18		42	
(as % of all delegates)		(29%)		(51%)
Incumbent Supervisors/Councilmen:				
Ran for Office[b]		. .	4[c]	
Elected	5		2[e]	
Previous Sup./Council Experience:				
Ran for Office[b]		. .	6[f]	
Elected	1		3[f]	

[a] In 1950, five incumbent legislators eliminated at primary, five at final election.
[b] Information for 1950 not available.
[c] Includes two incumbent councilmen who had previous legislative experience.
[d] Includes two former legislators who also had previous experience as supervisors.
[e] Includes one former legislator who was an incumbent councilman.
[f] Includes two incumbent legislators.

advantage, and the opprobrium tended to rub off on all irrespective of the type of district from which the legislator ran. As a result, legislators found they were conducting a more circumspect campaign than normally was their practice.

When the 1968 campaign was over and the votes counted, despite all the furor, incumbent legislators were elected on a four-to-one ratio, and among them accounted for 45 percent of the convention's membership. When their numbers were augmented by those delegates with prior legislative experience, they constituted a majority of the convention. Nevertheless, even though this was the result of a free election, the general public reaction against legislators' participation lingered on, and the political newcomers among the delegates continued to be suspicious of the legislators' motives. It was primarily because of this that the weight of the legislative component never could be mustered proportionate to its numerical superiority, and that the constitutional convention avoided procedures which might prove facilitative of the streamlined and (sometimes in Hawaii) steamroller tactics of a state legislature.

5.

Pre-Convention Preparations

Each constitutional convention is an ad hoc institution for which housing and staffing arrangements must be developed anew. The passage of time normally precludes the use of a predecessor's physical accommodations and personnel, although borrowing procedures help feed the illusion of a continuing body. Even where a convention is truly *sui generis*, however, without any predecessor in the state, the accumulated knowledge from constitutional conventions elsewhere counsels that certain preparatory steps be undertaken. For Hawaii's constitutional convention of 1950, to the extent the parallels of administering a legislature were inadequate, recourse was had to mainland practices. In 1968 the memory of the previous convention furnished strong guidelines, particularly with respect to the content of convention rules.

For the 1950 convention, general experience indicated the advisability of undertaking background data studies prior to the convening date. At the request of the Hawaii Statehood Commission, the Legislative Reference Bureau reported on the procedures and preparatory work involved. Its compiled *1950 Manual on State Constitutional Provisions* became the major resource for the convention delegates when deciding on the provisions of the new state constitution. All of this was eclipsed by the publications of the Legislative Reference Bureau in anticipation of the 1968 convention. Aided by a $20,000 preparatory appropriation, which was supplemented the next year by additional funds for printing, the bureau issued a series of 17 constitutional volumes. One study covered *Consti-*

tutional Convention Organization and Procedures, another 15 were arranged to correspond with the various articles of the 1950 constitution, and a general volume provided an introduction to the series and summaries for all of the constitutional articles. The near 2,000 pages of print touched on practically every matter which came before the convention, objectively mustering arguments pro and con on issues, and providing empirical data, legal opinion, and examples of constitutional phraseology obtained through a search of all 50 state constituent documents. Buttressed by this extensive research, delegates, before and after the convention got under way, had little need of other resource materials.

The Convention Site

In providing for the siting and setting up of the convention facilities, the Hawaii legislature was forewarned by an omission of 1950 when no one was legally charged with making advance arrangements. To fill the hiatus, Secretary Oren E. Long assumed responsibility and, through informal meetings with delegates, arrived at a series of satisfactory solutions. In 1968 the enabling legislation appropriating $1 million for defraying the pre-session, session and post-session expenses of the convention designated the office of the governor as recipient, or "the officers elected by the delegates if so designated by the Governor." And as to the site the 1967 legislation was even more specific: the convention was to convene "at a suitable place designated by the Governor."

Neither in 1950 nor 1968 was there an appropriate meeting place which satisfied all of the criteria desired for a constitutional convention: adequate space for delegates, staff and spectators; dignity befitting the undertaking; central location or at least ease of access; availability of parking for automobiles. The throne room of the venerable Iolani Palace could barely accommodate all 63 delegates in 1950, leaving practically no space for observers; in 1968 it was not thought feasible even to contemplate using the Palace. As substitute or supplement to the Palace in 1950, consideration was given to meeting in the adjoining Honolulu Armory or one of the Honolulu school auditoriums, such as McKinley High School. The final solution was to have brief opening and closing ceremonies in Iolani Palace, but otherwise conduct all business in the Armory, including the organization on opening day. The traditionalists were mollified while the pragmatists carried the day.

In 1968 the agreement finally reached on a convention site also was something of a compromise, again calling for the use of a barn-like structure. The situation presented was different, and the alternatives available greater. A state Capitol was now under construction, where the Armory once stood, and to many delegates the facilities available in the still uncompleted edifice provided the grandeur and spaciousness desired. But the governor was opposed, citing the $2,500 to $5,000 extra contractor's cost for each day's delay in construction, plus the uncertainty attendant on rehiring a work force once the construction could be renewed on conclusion of the convention. While indicating that he would take into account the views of the delegates, he proposed Kapiolani Community College, whose facilities were vacant during the summer, and referred to several other choices. To the delegates, selection of a school suggested a limited convention with a built-in deadline, for constitutional business would have to be completed before September when the schools opened.

An ad hoc committee of delegates investigated the various sites and, while concluding that the Kapiolani Community College facilities by themselves were not adequate, reluctantly concurred with the governor in eliminating the use of the state Capitol. Later, meeting with the delegates in caucus, the governor designated the adjoining McKinley High School gymnasium for plenary sessions, and the air-conditioned Kapiolani Community College building for delegates, staff offices and most committee meetings. Should the work of the convention not be finished by the time the school facilities were needed, quarters would be found elsewhere. As events were to prove, the return of the school premises remained as a subtle threat to the delegates, and the opening of the college was delayed a week to allow the convention to vacate the temporary offices. Even then it could not conclude its work and, after "making-do" in the gymnasium quarters, the convention finally moved to the old Senate chamber in Iolani Palace. The signing ceremony took place in the throne room, so once again the symbolism of the Palace legitimized Hawaii's constitution.

In perspective, the 1968 facilities were luxurious compared to the quarters occupied in 1950. Then the delegates enjoyed no private offices, staff was crowded together, and the rooms used for committee hearings proved noisy. True, offices in 1968 for the most part consisted of dividing classrooms into small cubicles by erecting temporary partitions, so delegates and their aides were crowded together, with little room for privacy. But they now had individual desks, private telephones, and an area to use as their own work space. Each of the officers had a separate room. The gymnasium quarters were not air-conditioned, and by afternoon the temperature contrasted noticeably with the coolness maintained in the college building, but they were not excessively uncomfortable. And even the acoustics were better in McKinley gymnasium, or so at least the "veteran" delegates reported.

Other Convention Preparations

With the conventions promising to be relatively short, equipment for both was borrowed from a number of governmental agencies, and most of the balance rented. The legislature was the source of much of the office furniture. For 1968 there had to be acquired some 200 desks, executive chairs for 82 delegates when meeting in plenary session, more than 150 typewriters, duplicating equipment, a public address system complete with desk microphones and recording equipment, an offset printing press, the Hawaii Senate podium, and even a broad expanse of canvas to cover the floor of the McKinley gymnasium so as not to damage the polished hardwood. All this was part of the duties of the Senate clerk, serving as aide of the president-elect, along with his responsibilities for supervising the $16,000 physical alterations of the convention offices. Unlike 1950, he was not requested to hang the hall with bunting to cover the drabness of that era's convention hall.

Supervision over central personnel fell to the clerk of the convention, to which post in 1968 the clerk of the House of Representatives was elected. Illustrative of the carryover of key personnel from legislature to convention, in 1950 the clerk of the Senate was chosen for this position, just as the legislatures' sergeant-at-arms held similar roles for both conventions. The 1950 convention, being strapped for funds, ran its affairs with a minimum personnel budget, although there was the suspicion that some of the 79 persons on the payroll were not necessarily there because they were essential in furthering the convention's work. "The extent to which patronage was used in the appointment of the employees of the 1950 convention cannot be gauged. It is evident that certain delegates did submit the names of persons desiring employment, but whether the President welcomed such recommendations from all delegates is not known." (Legislative Reference Bureau, "Constitutional Convention Organization and Procedures," *Hawaii Constitutional Studies,* 1968, page 38). There is no question about 1968, for the delegates openly shared patronage rights.

At the citizens' committee's symposium for delegates, legislative staff members voluntarily assisted in the distribution of materials, and it was taken for granted that they would be considered for positions with the convention. Later they aided at sessions of the pre-convention caucus. Once the president and other officers were designated by the caucus, the president named his administrative aide. After consultation with officers-designate, he likewise named other key convention staff, such as the sergeant-at-arms and attorneys. The two clerks of the legislature advised him on how many patronage posts were necessary for the conduct of the convention—printing staff, custodians, parking attendants, pages, etc.—and these were divided equally among the districts by random assignment. The district delegations then informally grouped and split up their largesse. Each delegate was also authorized to employ a stenographer and, if a committee chairman, to hire an additional stenographer and a committee clerk. Convention officers also received additional assistance. For the legislator-delegates, and the politically-aligned, there was no dearth of job seekers; some of the political newcomers among the delegates found it difficult to recruit persons desiring temporary work, even stenographers at the attractive rate of $31 a day.

All this is in sharp contrast with the penury of 1950, its central stenographic pool, and the clerks shared between committees. On the average day, three times as many staff members served the 1968 convention (220) as in 1950, and it proved difficult to find enough space to house them. The delegates were aware that they would be judged in part by the conduct of this large staff. Regardless of how hired, all convention staff were instructed to dress and behave decorously, in public situations address all delegates formally, and show the utmost courtesy to members of the public. Staff working directly for delegates took instructions from them, and kept such hours as they directed; many did little more than brew coffee, run personal errands for their delegates, and record telephone messages. The normal work week was six days; only specially designated staff was authorized to work on Sundays. At a pre-convention briefing, the assembled staff was also told that the services of the convention attorneys would primarily be directed to aiding the committees, while the Legislative Reference Bureau would respond to the drafting requests of the individual delegates. This last also contrasted with 1950 when, due to the paucity of convention staff, bureau personnel worked closely with committees as well as individuals, helped prepare committee proposals and their accompanying reports, and even drafted the Committee of the Whole reports.

Staffing did not begin firming until close to the convening time of both conventions. It waited on, as well as being a factor in the concluding of preliminary organizing maneuvers. The key element in these negotiations, both in 1950 and 1968, was the reaching of agreement on the person to be chosen as convention president. Other posts then fell into place, although in 1950 the number of vice presidents was not finally resolved until the delegates were sworn in and seated. Both conventions avoided any internecine struggle over choice of their presiding officer. There never was much question but that Samuel Wilder King would be president of the 1950 constitutional convention. He had been territorial delegate to the United States Congress, resigning to rejoin the Navy in World War II. The time he had given to the statehood cause had earned him the nickname of "the Statehood man." He was chairman of the Hawaii Statehood Commission, and also headed its State Constitution Committee at the time he filed for a convention seat. Prior to the elections he was being mentioned as a possible candidate, and his outright election at the primary strengthened his chances. It was rumored that thereafter he began seeking support, although he never openly announced his candidacy. The only other delegates prominently considered as potential rivals were both Democrats, and one took himself out of the running by announcing he preferred the chairmanship of the convention's Committee on Legislative Powers and Functions. The other eventually became one of the vice presidents. During this stage of pre-convention maneuvering, political party rivalries appeared, with the Democrats charging the Republicans were putting together a slate of officers for all key convention posts. Some Republicans argued that, as a majority of delegates was Republican, they should have the dominant voice in the organization and deliberations of the convention; the Democrats rejoined that the national administration and Congress were controlled by the Democratic Party, so to support statehood the Democrats should have a majority of the convention offices. But both factions supported King and, in view of his public announcements on convention structure which made him attractive to the independent delegates, his choice as president was assured. On the opening day of the convention he was unanimously elected, first as temporary chairman and then as permanent president.

Convention Officers, Rules and Organization

The pre-convention preparations could never resolve the matter of the remaining officers to the satisfaction of some of the minority Democrats. Since a Republican was to be president, they proposed a single vice president, a Democrat. Against the charge that the convention had been "rigged," and the key convention posts prearranged, the convention voted for four vice presidents, one from each county. The one Democrat from Kauai was elected unanimously, as were two of the other three Republican vice presidents. With Hebden Porteus elected as secretary, the Republicans had succeeded in capturing five of the top offices; one went to a Democrat and none to the Independents.

In 1968 the selection of president proceeded with almost as great dispatch, again with interparty political rivalries playing no major role. Now, though, it was intraparty stresses within the majority Democratic delegation which led to the choice of a Republican, a decision which embodied the political risk of moving him a step closer to occupying the state's governorship.

Having served as secretary of the first convention, a long-time legislator and currently Senate Republican minority leader, Hebden Porteus was early mooted as a potential president for the second convention. After his election from a single-member, grouped-precinct district, some of the Republican delegates began campaigning on his behalf. Following the pattern set previously by King, Porteus did not publicly announce his candidacy for the post but indicated his availability. Like King, who secured the support of the Independent delegates by his stand on committees, Porteus, shortly after his election, asked all delegates to consider creation of about as many committees as functioned in 1950. In addition, in his letter he suggested a range of procedural provisions which indicated he favored a free and open convention. He thereby reassured the nonprofessionals among the delegates that he was not to be numbered among those legislator-delegates who were being accused of plotting a convention to be run like a legislature, with gag limitations on proposal and debate. Later, this group decided it included no qualified candidate among its membership, and in caucus gave the bulk of its vote to Porteus.

But what elected Porteus to the presidency was a bitter division among the Democrats in the state Senate, with the two protagonists now both present as delegates. Since the state elections were to be held in a few more months, the Democratic party could ill afford to allow a recurrence of the Senate struggle in a new setting. Apart from party fortunes, the delegates were sensitive to the public relations image of the convention, having been informed that contributing to the recent defeat of the New York and Rhode Island revisions was the negative spectacle that both conventions made of themselves. Agreement on a Republican, particularly one committed to conducting the convention in a fully open manner, avoided the holding of both the party and the convention to public censure. A coalition composed of Republicans, Democrats identified with the Burns/ILWU faction, and non-professionals combined to designate Senator Porteus as president-elect, the minority reportedly mustering only 16 votes in opposition.

Senator Porteus' letter to all delegates had stressed the necessity for organization of the convention prior to its opening date. Well he might, for he personally knew how failure to hold preparatory caucuses had delayed the work of the 1950 convention. Then, a week before convening, eight Oahu delegates informally met to develop organizing proposals. Among them were King and three other non-legislators, and four incumbent legislators, including Porteus. They relied on the Missouri and New Jersey convention rules as models, adapting them to the Hawaiian situation and agreeing that their adoption should not be attempted on the first day. The convention would operate on suggested temporary rules, while a special 17-member committee debated over the suggested draft and proposed the convention's permanent rules. The eight-man rump group could not agree on the number of either vice presidents or committees to recommend, presaging the fight over vice presidents which occurred on the convention's opening day.

It was not until the third day of the 1950 convention that the committee-drafted permanent rules were submitted. During the interim the tentative rules were revised, the committee also referring to the rules of the territorial House of Representatives. Even then the convention was not ready to accept all of the 65 proposed rules and, after adopting the first 15 pertaining to the officers, held the balance for study during the Easter recess. A full week after convening, the permanent rules were approved and the convention's committees finally appointed.

The 1968 convention enjoyed advantages in organizing not afforded in 1950. The calling of a symposium for the delegates-elect by the citizens' committee provided a ready-made opportunity to bring the delegates together in Honolulu for caucusing a month in advance of convening. The governor's willingness to release convention funds to permit the delegates-elect to receive their per diem while at the caucus encouraged a large attendance. The state enabling legislation declared that the delegate elected from the first representative district should serve as temporary convention chairman, so that he had putative authority to issue the call for the caucus and to preside on calling it to order. And, of greatest importance, the rules of the 1950 convention required only minor modification to be applicable *holus bolus* for the year 1968.

Once called to order, with minor opposition the caucus elected Porteus as caucus chairman. Thereafter he played a preeminent role, both helping to shape the convention organization and molifying the suspicion with which the non-professionals regarded each move of the legislator-delegates. His first major act was to name a 13-member arrangements committee, auspiciously balanced to have at least one delegate from each of the state's eight senatorial districts, six legislator-delegates (and with Porteus meeting with the committee, they would constitute exactly half), four delegates beside himself with experience in the 1950 convention, the delegate spokesman for the non-professional group, a representative of the female contingent, the speaker of the House of Representatives, and both contenders for leadership in the state Senate. Six of the seven convention officers later to be elected (besides the president) were on the committee! As a fitting capstone for this adroitly selected committee, its party composition closely approximated that of the convention. The major charge of the arrangements committee was not the direction it received to recommend a convention site, but to prepare the convention rules for caucus scrutiny.

By the time the caucus next met two weeks later, a set of proposed rules had been drafted and distributed among the delegates. They were substantially the same as those adopted by the 1950 convention, and changes were mainly concerned with safeguarding full deliberation in the Committee of the Whole, and assuring that issues could not be buried in standing committee. The special committee proposed expressly to preclude motions to lay on the table any previous question in the Committee of the Whole. The caucus not only approved, but included the motion to postpone indefinitely within the ban. The caucus concurred that an 82-member convention had to allow each delegate less time for speaking, so agreed with the reduction to 10 minutes for the first time (in 1950, 15 minutes) and five on the second, but took solace in the knowledge that it would now be harder to adopt a previous question motion to cut off debate in plenary session (two-thirds vote, instead of the 1950 majority of delegates present). Although the caucus accepted with some skepticism the suggested provision permitting 25 delegates to recall a proposal from committee, this was in good part because it had earlier insisted that the rules expressly state that in Committee of the Whole, during consideration of a standing committee proposal, all matters on the same subject were to be in order. Should a particular proposal be bottled up in standing committee, it could always be brought to the attention of the whole convention in the form of an amendment to the proposal before the delegates.

Much of the rules was devoted to establishing the convention structure, its officers and committees. Here, and in specifying how the work of the convention was to proceed, the 1950 rules were almost wholly borrowed for use by the 1968 convention. In place of 1950's four vice presidents the caucus, after much debate, adopted the original recommendation in the committee's proposed rules that there be five, with two from the city and county of Honolulu. Some delegates desired a "working convention," and proposed to eliminate recognition for the Neighbor Islands by cutting down on the number of vice presidents. Others feared that if this group of officers grew too large, it would become a *de facto* steering body which might control patronage and convention policy. Porteus' statement that he would not name any vice president to a standing committee chairmanship went far to reassure the non-professional delegates that the convention would remain open, and helped carry the day for five vice presidents. The post of assistant secretary was also added by the caucus. Not by coincidence, the convention officers now totaled eight, equal to the number of senatorial districts in the state.

In its recommendations on committees, the temporary caucus committee partially negated the pre-election statements of Porteus by reducing their number to 12 standing and two administrative committees. One new committee was recommended, splitting the 1950 Committee on Legislative Powers and Functions to create a separate group which could give

CONVENTION COMMITTEES AND THEIR SIZE

1950		1968	
Bill of Rights	(15)	Bill of Rights, Suffrage & Elec.	(23)
Suffrage and Elections	(7)		
Legis. Powers & Functions	(15)	Legislative Powers & Functions	(23)
		Legislative App. & Districting	(23)
Exec. Powers & Functions	(15)	Executive	(23)
Judiciary	(15)	Judiciary	(23)
Taxation and Finance	(15)	Taxation & Finance	(23)
Local Government	(15)	Local Government	(23)
Education	(15)	Public Health, Ed. & Welfare;	
Health & Public Welfare	(11)	Labor & Industry	(23)
Industry and Labor	(11)		
Ag., Conservation & Land	(11)	Agriculture, Conservation, Land	
Hawaiian Homes Com. Act	(9)	& Hawaiian Homes	(23)
Rev., Amend., Init., Ref.		Revision, Amend., & Other Prov.	(23)
and Recall	(11)		
Ordinances & Continuity of Law	(7)		
Miscellaneous Matters	(9)		
Style	(15)	Style	(17)
Submission & Information	(15)	Submission & Information	(16)
Rules & Order of Business	(9)	Rules	(15)
Accounts	(7)	Accounts & Printing	(15)
Printing	(7)		

its full attention to the *raison d'être* of the convention, legislative apportionment and districting. The remaining committees were either parallels or represented combinations of their 1950 predecessors.

The respective committee sizes in the two conventions gives some indication of how the temporary caucus committee anticipated distribution of the workload in 1968. It also reflects the political reality that delegates require recognition in the form of committee assignments, but creating committees just for that purpose threatened to prolong unduly the work of the convention and inflate the bulk of the constitution with busy-work amendments. As first proposed the standing committees in 1968 would have had only 21 members each, but, in the endeavor to satisfy as many delegates' committee choices as possible, they were increased to 23, and the Style Committee to 17. Also, the Submission and Information Committee had as ex-officio members the convention officers and the chairmen of the other 11 subject matter committees, a membership which proved unwieldly and so prestigious as to greatly delay the committee when it reached the crucial stage of decision making.

Once the caucus expressed its approval of the proposed 1968 convention rules, the naming of officers began. Senator Porteus was elected as president-designate, now unanimously. To the delegates of each county was assigned the responsibility of choosing their vice president; on Oahu a runoff from a field of 11 candidates named two officers-elect. For the positions of secretary and assistant secretary, only delegates from Oahu were nominated, so that five posts out of the top eight were filled from Honolulu. Designations completed, it was found that legislators and non-legislators had divided the offices equally, as had the two political parties, and each of the state's eight senatorial districts had captured one key post. The mechanism by which this was achieved was visible to all: Senator Porteus hailed from the 6th senatorial; the speaker of the House, coming from a district within the 7th, was elected to the post of secretary; next a delegate from the 5th senatorial was chosen assistant clerk. In the Oahu runoff, delegates from the 3rd and 4th senatorial districts won over two others resident in senatorial districts already having key convention officers. A delay in naming Hawaii County's vice president was reputedly settled only by one of the contenders receiving a committee chairmanship.

Two weeks later the delegates reassembled in caucus to hear the final details on the convening ceremonies only two days off, and to learn of their committee assignments. Just as President King had done 18 years earlier, President-elect Porteus took into consideration the delegates' expressed preferences and technical qualifications, and also attempted to provide both partisan and geographic balance. In addition, he now had an opportunity to narrow the breach between legislator-delegate and non-legislator, which he proceeded to do by giving the latter a majority in 10 of the 12 standing committees. The committee chairmanships were evenly allotted between the two groups, as were the vice chairman posts. In 1950 the Republicans had captured the constitutional convention and organized it accordingly. Now the Democrats were in the majority, and Porteus recognized this by having Democrats chair nine committees; Independents, two; and Republicans, three. In every one of the 14 committees, Democrats had sufficient membership to control, even when a Republican had been assigned the committee chairmanship. For the politically-sensitive chairmanship of the Legislative Apportionment and Districting Committee, Porteus named an Independent. For the equally legislative-sensitive chairmanship of the Legislative Powers and Functions Committee he chose a non-legislator. The distribution of committee leadership posts proportionately matched the ethnic composition of the convention, the small Filipino segment excepted. Only one delegate publicly expressed dissatisfaction with his assignments; several from Oahu exchanged committee memberships, under the stricture that all exchanges so made must be within the county delegation, so as not to disturb the Oahu-Neighbor Island balance.

CONVENTION COMMITTEE MEMBERSHIP, 1968

	Legislative Composition				Political Party			Neigh. Islands	1950 Deleg.
	Ch.	V. Ch.	Leg.	Non-leg.	Dem.	Rep.	Ind.		
Agriculture	X	—	10	13	17	5	1	5	2
Bill of Rights	—	X	10	13	17	6	—	4	3
Executive	X	—	11	12	16	6	1	5	1
Judiciary	—	—	8	15	13	10	—	7	3
Leg. App.	—	X	11	12	14	7	2	6	1
Leg. Powers	—	X	10a	13a	15	6	2	5	1
Local Gov't.	X	—	10	13	15	8	—	7	2
Public Health	X	X	10	13	20	3	—	5	2
Revision, etc.	X	—	13	10	18	5	—	7	2
Style	—	X	6	11	11	4	2	4	1
Submission, etc.	—	X	6	10	11	5	—	1	1
Taxation	—	X	11b	12b	17	5	1	5	2
Accounts	X	—	8c	7c	11	4	—	4	—
Rules	X	—	11	4	14	1	—	4	1

[a] Legislative Powers originally had 11 legislator-delegates, but one was replaced by a non-legislator.

[b] Taxation originally had 12 legislator-delegates, but one was replaced by a non-legislator.

[c] Accounts originally had eight non-legislator delegates, but one was replaced by a legislator-delegate.

The distribution of committee assignments discloses several anomalies, patently revealing that the balance President-elect Porteus sought in other committees was deliberately being ignored. The Rules Committee's Republican chairman was flanked by 14 Democrats, while he and 10 others were legislators. If they were of a mind to do so, the Democrats/legislator-delegates would be in position to make the convention consider changes in the rules agreed on in caucus. The Judiciary Committee, the only one with both a Republican chairman and vice chairman, neither of whom were legislator-delegates, had more Republican members and fewer legislator-delegates than any other major committee. Its quotas of Neighbor Islanders and delegates elected to the 1950 convention were not exceeded in any other committee. The controversy shaping up over adopting the "merit plan" for selecting Hawaii's judges was adumbrated in the membership of this committee. But how to explain the designation of five (out of eight) women delegates to vice chairman offices? Was this a mark of chivalry, or did it correctly measure the little more than titular prestige lodged in the office?

6.

The Convention Opens

History does not report in detail the advance preparations made for opening the 1950 constitutional convention. Most likely, once the 26-stage procedure of the convening ceremonies was agreed to in advance, the secretary of the territory and then the temporary chairman responded to delegates, improvising their words as the general outline was followed. In 1968 nothing was left to chance and on the opening day the delegates rarely deviated from a prepared scenario which assigned a part in *haec verba* to each one of the 82 members assembled. The delegate from the first representative district had been empowered by the caucus to make the necessary arrangements for the convention's opening, in line with the statutory direction that he call the convention to order. In his name, and that of the president-designate, invitations were sent, space assigned and provision made to accommodate the guests. With the slate of officers already prearranged and the permanent rules drawn by the caucus, the convention quickly organized, named its officers, appointed committees and was ready for work. Because it was so planned, the first proposal had to wait only until the next day for introduction. The parallel activities of the 1950 convention took nearly a full week to complete.

Both conventions met amidst flowers and pageantry, each delegate the recipient of numerous leis and flower pieces with which he adorned his neck and desk, respectively. Representatives of the mass media recorded the spectacle in picture and word. A distinguished panel of honored guests, a larger gathering of families and friends of delegates, and a still greater crowd of a thousand or so members of the general public were present to witness each convention convene. In the case of the first, it was under a huge banner proclaiming "HAWAII—49th State." Time was to reveal that the endeavor at constitution drafting was to be an important milestone along the path to statehood, but Alaska was to be admitted into the Union first, and to become the 49th state.

The Convention Structure

The seating arrangements for delegates grouped each county separately, nominally to facilitate intra-delegation communications. It had the unfortunate effect of physically emphasizing the Neighbor Island-Oahu dichotomy. In 1968, within the county configurations delegates were seated alphabetically, which enabled the clerks to check the empty desks each morning and record absences, dispensing with the necessity of a lengthy daily roll call. Administrative convenience would have been served even more if the convention were arranged entirely that way, irrespective of county.

As provided in the rules, the permanent officers elected for both conventions were a president, vice president for each county, and secretary. The 1968 convention added an assistant secretary, and a second vice president for the city and county of Honolulu, but, both formally and actually, the delineation of duties shared between the officers as first declared in the 1950 rules remained much the same. The president presided over sessions of the convention, preserving order, holding the delegates to the issue before them, and declaring the vote and announcing the results on all questions and decisions. He referred proposals, petitions and other convention documents to the appropriate committee. Each time the convention sat as a committee of the whole, the president named the chairman to preside over it. Although nowhere so specified, administrative, clerical and custodial activities were supervised by staff reporting to him. Together with the secretary, he certified all official acts and all vouchers for the payment of convention expenses. This was more than a nominal act, for it symbolized that he was responsible for the legality of all final convention decisions as well as the reasonableness of all convention administrative actions. His real power flowed from his selection by the delegates as the one person charged with providing cohesion to the convention and with furnishing the leadership necessary to keep the convention moving. The rules declared that the president was an ex-officio member without vote on all committees, but this technicality was probably unnecessary, for if they had been silent on the subject, his status among the delegates would most likely have enabled him to participate in committee deliberations.

In the temporary absence of the president his duties and responsibilities devolved from day to day on one of the vice presidents. There was no intent to confer seniority on any of them, which was disclosed by the requirement that the vice presidents take turns in serving; at the 1950 convention, priority was in the numerical order of the senatorial districts, while the 1968 rules specified the alphabetical sequence of their names. In the case of vacancy in the office of president the convention would have elected a new officer. For the most part the substitution of the vice president applied only to presiding at plenary sessions of the convention in the absence of the president.

The secretary supervised the keeping of the convention journal and, under the direction of the president, prepared the daily calendar of convention business. Similarly it was his responsibility to see that proposals were correctly numbered, records kept and materials properly printed. The actual execution of these tasks was delegated to the chief clerk. The one duty which could not be so shifted was the certification of official acts, documents and vouchers. The creation of the new post of assistant secretary made it possible to delegate responsibility to him for the adjustment of space allocations, the coordination of committee meetings, the assignment of meeting-room facilities and comparable scheduling chores.

On organizing the convention in 1950, and following the selection of officers, five staff members were also elected by majority vote of the delegates: chief clerk, assistant clerk, chaplain and two sergeants-at-arms. The 1968 rules cut these to the first two named. Chaplains still were called on each day to give the invocation, but the convention adopted the practice which had evolved in the House of Representatives since the 1950 convention of requesting the services of clergy from differing religions and denominations. The recent Hawaii convention is probably the only one in the United States to have had Buddhist, Christian and Jewish chaplains ask for spiritual guidance to its work. At the 1968 convention, there were also a sergeant-at-arms and his deputies, but all were appointed by the president.

Completing the convention structure were both the permanent substantive and administrative committees created in the rules and the ad hoc committees. At the 1950 convention a total of 234 appointments was made by the president to the 20 permanent committees, or an average of almost four per delegate. While the number of committee posts ranged around this median, one delegate received six committee assignments, and at the other extreme the president and secretary each had only one. The total number of committee posts at the 1968 convention rose to 293, notwithstanding that committees were reduced by almost a third. The median number of committee assignments per delegate remained about the same but with the range of variation from the midpoint sharply reduced. Neither the president, secretary nor assistant secretary was appointed as a member of any committee in 1968, but all participated in committee deliberations as if the rules relating to the ex-officio committee status of the president had expressly included the other two officers.

As was to be expected, with fewer committees at the 1968 convention and each with more members, the problem of overlapping membership was exacerbated and the scheduling of meetings became more difficult. Every committee shared at least a third of its membership with another, and sometimes several other committees. The Executive Committee could never meet separately at an hour set for the Taxation and Finance Committee, as the same 10 members sat on both. When, toward the latter part of the session, the Committee on Style began functioning, the Committee on Revision, Amendment and Other Provisions of necessity could not, for the same members comprised a majority of both. Not all of this proved dysfunctional, for in such cases as the Committees on Executive/Taxation and Finance or on Legislative Powers/Legislative Apportionment, their jurisdictions obviously overlapped and coordination was facilitated by their joint membership.

The Committees

All of the standing committees had multiple functions. Each substantive committee was responsible not only for deliberating and reporting on every specific proposal introduced by the delegates and referred to it, but also for that portion of the constitution encompassed within the scope of its title. At the 1950 convention, with the constitution yet to be framed, the latter assignment was more nebulous than in 1968, when the articles of the constitution could be parceled out among the committees. The Committee on Style rephrased and rearranged proposals in proper order prior to their final passage without authority to change the sense or purpose of any proposal. In addition it served the function of a legislative "Third Reading File Committee," calling the attention of the convention to conflicts between proposals ready for consideration on the floor of the convention and others already acted on favorably. The Committee on Submission and Information also had a dual responsibility.

One of its functions pertained to recommendations to the convention on the form and manner in which to submit the constitution to the people. The other was concerned with making sure that the public was kept advised of what was transpiring during the course of the convention and, on adjournment, to educate the voters on the constitutional provisions they would be called on to approve. Even the Rules Committee in the 1968 convention did more than consider and report on changes in organization and rules. "Miscellaneous" resolutions not within the jurisdiction of other committees were treated by the president as falling within its jurisdiction. And the last of the committees, Accounts and Printing, encompassed the work assigned to two separate committees at the 1950 convention.

Three temporary committees served the 1950 constitutional convention, this beside the purely nominal committees appointed to escort visitors to the rostrum and perform other honorific and routine chores. On convening, the rules of the first convention were drafted by such an ad hoc committee; another investigated the qualifications of a delegate, terminating in his removal from office; and the third was appointed to confer with Congress on statehood matters. No need for comparable committees arose at the 1968 convention. The closest to these temporary bodies was the president's designation of all female delegates as an informal committee to advise him on social matters pertinent to the convention; its one announced contribution was the scheduling of a picnic-style outing for the delegates.

Powers and Liabilities of Convention Membership

As part of the first day's ceremonies, the delegates took the oath of office required of all public officers. In 1950 they also subscribed to the loyalty oath prescribed by the legislature for officers and employees. Today these both read almost identically, but that was not the situation in 1950 when, in step with the McCarthy era, the loyalty oath also included express denials of membership in suspect organizations and other subversive actions and beliefs. Interestingly, the more stringent 1950 provisions did not stop one delegate from admittedly taking the loyalty oath falsely (he later resigned, after explaining the reasons for his actions) or furnish the grounds for removal of a second delegate who refused to answer the questions asked of him by a subcommittee of the U. S. House of Representatives' UnAmerican Activities Committee. The delegates by more than a two-thirds vote concluded that the latter was disqualified from continuing to sit in the convention because of his "contumacious

conduct before and toward the . . . [U. S. Committee] and this constitutional convention of 1950. . . ." Both vacant positions were filled by
gubernatorial appointments of the defeated runner-up candidates.

This action in removing a member illustrates the power held by the
convention over its membership lodged in the convention, including the
authority to preserve its own decorum and take disciplinary action against
delegates who commit breaches of that decorum or who are disorderly.
How far the convention's process extended to non-delegates remained un-
tested both in 1950 and in 1968. To fill part of the hiatus, the state legislature conferred on the latter convention all powers exercised by state
legislative committees. This granted the 1968 convention power to take
testimony and obtain records under subpoena, and also to discipline
recalcitrant witnesses. Whether the convention could exercise sanctions
against non-delegates for breaches of prescribed behavior or disorderly
conduct remained moot. Fortunately for convention harmony, neither
body was called on to discipline any non-delegate, and 1968 saw no
repetition of the 1950 convention's traumatic disqualifying of a delegate.

The personal legal liability of the delegates to non-delegates for actions
taken remained as uncertain as the extent of the convention's authority
over non-delegates. The state legislature, in providing for the 1968 convention, granted delegates the same privilege from arrest as afforded
legislators, and also the same salary and per diem rates, but did not
include reference to the legal immunities which the legislator enjoys
while in the exercise of his legislative functions. How far the delegates
might be subject to suits for libel and slander would, therefore, be determined under the general rules applicable to all public officers. Insofar
as could be ascertained, in both conventions the delegates set about their
duties oblivious to the possible legal liability involved.

The Convention's Duration

The 1950 convention convened with the knowledge that it was expected
to be in session for at least 60 work-days. The last quarterly installment
of the delegate's compensation ($1,000 in all) would not be disbursed
until the sixtieth day of the convention, excluding Sundays and holidays.
No comparable limitation was written into the 1968 appropriation, so that
the delegates could have received the total $2,500 stipend immediately
and then adjourned. Of course such action was never contemplated by
the delegates, but the length of the convention was paramount in their
minds and a 45-day deadline was publicly broached. The day before the
July 15 convening, the sergeant-at-arms in the staff briefing period simi-

larly expressed the hope that the convention would terminate by the end of August. During the opening day's ceremonies, the tone was one of efficiency and dispatch. At the meeting of committee chairmen which followed on that day, President Porteus was importuned to announce a timetable with a specific endpoint, even if only tentative, toward which the convention could aim. He refused, but made it evident that he did not consider that the convention would be a protracted one.

Few delegates desired to duplicate the approximately three and one-half months' duration of the 1950 convention. Many had to begin campaigning in September for the October primary election, and favored the 1968 convention's concluding its deliberations long before then. The pressure to get done was obvious from the day the convention convened. It was only the minority which, like the delegate's private letter of protest circulated among the members of the convention, expressed lack of "sympathy with those who wish a speedy adjournment or with those who would impose time limitations on our deliberations." Nevertheless, it was they, together with anticipated voter rejection of a product publicly castigated as having been "railroaded" through the convention, which discouraged any overt action to truncate the 1968 convention. Well before its convening date, a newspaper commentator estimated that two and one-half months might be a realistically adequate time within which to complete the convention's work. On the day that the convention opened, this appeared too optimistically long. In fact, despite internal pressures for a rapid adjournment, the length of the convention's life was closely to approximate this estimate.

7.

The Convention at Work

From the outset the 1950 and 1968 conventions established almost identical procedures for considering constitutional proposals. On first impression they were similar to the procedures which might be observed by a single-house legislature in enacting bills, although they were necessarily more complicated at the concluding stages. The similarities grow more tenuous when the underlying process is examined. The vehicle used by the conventions for taking substantive action was technically called a "proposal," rather than borrowing the term "bill" from legislative usage. Proposals could be introduced by one or more delegates, or by a committee. Normally the individual legislator went to the Legislative Reference Bureau or the attorney general to have his ideas put into proper form, and to "expert" drafts originating with private groups; committees usually used the services of the convention's attorneys. "Pre-filing" of proposals ensured that a large number would be on hand, ready for introduction on the first day of regular business.

Upon introduction, numbering and pro forma first reading by title, all proposals were ordered printed and normally referred to an appropriate standing committee. Those encompassing more than one constitutional subject might receive joint referral to two or more committees. The committees then studied the proposals, invited experts to testify, scheduled public hearings where a broader range of views might be expressed, amassed a background of pertinent fact and opinion, deliberated and

submitted their reports to the convention. These committee proceedings
—both public hearings called after a minimum of two days' notice and the
general committee meetings—were open to the public and representatives
of all the mass media.

The standing committee was faced with three options. If the subject
matter was not appropriate to the committee's jurisdiction it could recommend referral to another standing committee; this rarely occurred. If the
proposal was found unsatisfactory the committee could report it out
with the recommendation that it be filed, which effectively spelled its
death; this was the fate of the bulk of proposals which never found their
way into the constitution. The third option was to prepare a substitute
committee proposal if the delegate's proposal was defective in some way,
or ought be combined with the suggestions of other delegates. The filing
of the delegate's proposal would be recommended in the committee report to which the committee proposal was then attached. Logically there
is a fourth option, but it was never exercised. Even if a delegate's proposal was found satisfactory and sufficiently comprehensive it was always
treated under the third option, so that none was ever reported on favorably for adoption in either convention. With the delegate's proposal filed,
all further convention action centered around the committee proposal
which was numbered separately and recorded in a different series. Standing committee reports based on either of the first two options were usually adopted by the convention without referral to the Committee of the
Whole. The remaining reports lay on the table for a day, and then the
motion to adopt the report constituted passage on first reading of the
attached committee proposal. A minimum of four days after both were
returned from the printer they were ready for placement on the calendar
for convention consideration.

Consideration of Committee Proposals

To provide maximum scope for debate and the greatest degree of in-
formality, most of the discussion on a committee proposal was held in
Committee of the Whole where cloture could not be moved under the
1968 rules, and by tacit agreement was not used in 1950. After it had been
fully considered, and most likely amended, the Committee of the Whole
would rise and the convention sit again in plenary session. At this time an
oral committee progress report would be delivered with the request that
leave be granted to file a full written report. Upon the printing of the
Committee of the Whole's report, including, if necessary, an amended
draft of the committee proposal, motion would be made in plenary ses-

sion to adopt the report. This also had the effect of adopting the standing committee's proposal if the Committee of the Whole approved it without change, or accepting it with the exceptions proposed by the Committee of the Whole now incorporated into an amended form of the committee proposal. At this stage any delegate could object, and again propose amendments, possibly the same amendments which had been rejected previously in the Committee of the Whole. Once adoption had been voted the committee proposal had passed second reading, and was referred to the Committee on Style. Beyond second reading, no substantive amendment could be offered on the floor of the convention without the unanimous consent of the delegates present, and this was seldom granted.

Within five convention days, the Committee on Style reported on all proposals sent to it. Changes might be made in phraseology, grammar, arrangement and language, and accompanying them would be a report containing the reasons for committee action. The report and the rearranged proposal would be returned to the convention for printing and consideration at plenary session. Disagreement could be voiced at this stage and, should amendments be adopted on the floor to change the phraseology, the amended proposal technically would be again referred to the Committee on Style for further review, report and reprinting. To speed up the process the rules would sometimes be suspended to permit a subcommittee of the Style Committee to examine the changes on the spot and concur in the amendments.

After 48-hours' notice made in plenary session, third reading occurred. The secretary would have prepared the proposal in final form, his name affixed to each page of the official copy. At this stage, if requested by any delegate, the proposal would be read at length. Adoption required the affirmative vote of a majority of the membership with the vote taken by roll call and recorded.

Although now passed, the proposal was referred back once again to the Committee on Style for proper arrangement in the constitution with the other proposals. The committee as its last act reported to the convention on the final form of the constitution and all the amendments proposed to be made. Acceptance of this report by the convention in plenary session also required the affirmative vote of a majority of the membership.

Two major stages remained before the proposals were ready for voter action. The final form of the constitution next went to the Committee on Submission and Information, which recommended the method and manner of submitting it to the people. Once the committee's resolution was passed by a majority of the convention membership, the final draft con-

stitution was signed by the president, secretary and the concurring delegates. Lest this last stage be thought of as automatic, one of the delegates
in 1950 initially refused to sign and then was granted permission to reconsider, while another never did affix her signature because of objections
to provisions on the Hawaiian Homes Commission.

This lengthy process was designed to slow down convention action and
assure full consideration in both committee and general session. At each
crucial stage the delegate was guaranteed sufficient time to permit full
study before voting. For final decision making by the whole convention,
majority consensus was the minimum. Requirements of printing and
notice furnished additional safeguards. After all it was a constitution
which was being written, and there was no margin for error.

The delegates said nothing formally in their rules about adopting resolutions, but the seeming parallels with a legislature easily aided the transfer of the practice. Their use was acknowledged from the outset, as resolutions facilitated the convening process. Non-controversial resolutions
were adopted on introduction and then printed for distribution. Others
were printed and referred to a committee, where they either died or were
reported out with recommendation. At the 1968 convention their use for
other than formal purposes was discouraged; of the 36 resolutions introduced three were adopted on the first day, opening the convention,
and three on the last day, preparatory to winding up convention business.

The Order of Business

The convention normally followed the same order of business each day.
On calling the convention to order, and giving the invocation, the president announced that the secretary had read the journal, prepared by the
clerk, and that it was duly executed and signed. There was no reading at
length of the journal before the plenary session. At the 1950 convention,
roll call had preceded the journal "reading," but in 1968 this was replaced by the clerk visually determining that a quorum was present and
so advising the president.

Next followed presentation of petitions, memorials and communications,
reports of standing and select committees, and the introduction and first
readings of proposals. The reference of proposals to committees and the
taking up or referral, as appropriate, of motions and resolutions followed,
and the convention then turned to any unfinished business on its calendar.
The last would include any matter which had been made a special order
for a previous day but had not been reached and therefore carried over
under the order of unfinished business to the next succeeding day. A

majority vote of the delegates present could adopt a motion for placing on special order.

During the first part of the 1968 convention, plenary sessions met in the morning, quickly disposed of their business and adjourned to allow the committees to begin work. The 1950 convention adopted a later morning convening time. In both conventions, as the standing committees began reporting substantive proposals, more and more time each day was spent in general session on the "general orders of the day." The sequence prescribed for the general orders was: consideration by Committee of the Whole, reports of the Committee of the Whole, standing committee reports and proposals reported from standing committees, second reading, action on reports as to arrangement and phraseology from the Committee on Style, and third reading and roll call vote. All of this was recorded on electronic tape, rather than being reproduced verbatim in the daily journal. The journal consisted of a concise statement of all matters brought before the convention, and the action taken. With statehood, the daily journal for the entire convention and supporting convention documents were printed. At the same time the proceedings of the Committee of the Whole were transcribed and published. Presumably the records of the 1968 constitutional convention will receive comparable publication.

The parliamentary procedure observed corresponded with average, general legislative practice. The majority of the convention constituted a quorum and, except where provision was made in the rules to the contrary, a majority of the quorum was sufficient for taking affirmative action. Delegates were permitted to raise questions of personal privilege, points of order and requests for information. Should the outcome of a voice vote be questionable, a delegate could call for a division of the house, whereupon the president again put the question and the ayes and noes would be counted by a rising vote. Whenever 10 delegates so requested, a roll call was used and the votes entered in the journal. Hawaii allowed a delegate the right of *kanalua*, that is, to remain silent the first time his name was called by the clerk; after the roll had been completed, if he remained silent on the next call of his name his vote was recorded as affirmative.

The rules at both conventions specified the requisite minimum votes on designated matters. For the most part they read identically.

To facilitate the work of the convention, the attorneys prepared digests of proposals and the Legislative Reference Bureau compiled a weekly cumulative index. Supplementing the latter was a status table showing the action taken on all proposals and resolutions, and cross references to committee reports. At the 1968 convention a running table on sections of

MINIMUM VOTES REQUIRED ON SELECTED MATTERS

	1950	1968
Suspension of rules	maj.[a]	2/3 present[b]
Amendment or repeal of rules	maj.	maj.[a]
Suspension or removal of members	2/3[c]	2/3[c]
Previous question	maj. present[d]	2/3 present
Passage on third reading & final reading	maj.	maj.
Adoption of submission resolution	maj.	maj.
Amendment to proposal on third reading	unan.[e]	unan.[e]
Recall of proposal from committee	....	25

[a] Majority in 1950 was 32 delegates; in 1968 it was 42 delegates.
[b] A quorum being 42, minimum was 28 delegates.
[c] In 1950, 42 delegates; in 1968, 55.
[d] In 1950, 16 delegates.
[e] Minimum of 32 in 1950, 42 in 1968.

the constitution affected was also published. The digests were distributed solely for the use of committees to which the proposals were referred, but the index and status tables were available for general use.

Procedure in Committees

The convention rules did not detail standing committee procedure. As each committee organized, the chairman indicated the manner in which he proposed to conduct meetings and these became the guidelines observed, supplemented by the normal applicable principles of parliamentary procedure. It was not unusual, however, for a chairman to refuse to entertain a motion to lay on the table until all members had a full opportunity for debate. Those committee chairmen who had legislative experience tended to borrow heavily from legislative practices. As an example, in 1968 one announced that, after a quorum was obtained on organizing, his committee would recess from meeting to meeting so that the problem would never arise of having to demonstrate the presence of a quorum to commence a wholly new meeting. The nature of the committee minutes and records likewise varied, depending on the skills of their chairmen and staff. The greater financial resources of the 1968 convention permitted the presence of secretaries, clerks and recording equipment, and the minutes maintained for the committees could now be very complete. In those committees for which extensive data compilations had to be prepared, the larger staffing of the 1968 convention proved particularly valuable. Unfortunately, given the increased financial outlay for staff in 1968, more attorneys than the three appointed by the convention could have been used by the committees to good advantage.

Nominally, committees held two types of sessions: public hearings and regular committee meetings. The former received greater advance publicity but the latter were also open meetings and members of the public attending were frequently allowed to present statements, so that there was no sharply delineated distinction. When the committees reached the stage of decision making the public was no longer welcome to volunteer comments, although, significantly, this did not take place in executive session and the process was observable by everyone.

At the 1968 convention, the roles of the committee chairmen differed markedly. It soon became evident to most chairmen that one of their most important functions was to lead their committees in understanding the elements of the decisions which they would be called on to make. If he was not already so equipped, this required each chairman to quickly master a broad factual background; a few never succeeded in this and found themselves losing control over their committees. Some chairmen supported specific policy positions, becoming if not open at least tacit advocates in their committees; at the other extreme, some chairmen did little more than set the agenda for the next meeting and preside. The impression gained from observing both types of leadership was that greater committee identity and cohesiveness developed under a strong chairman, even when the committee could conclude its work only by splitting into divergent majority and minority positions; the style of the permissive chairman seemed to encourage the members to proceed on their own tangents, with the result that it became difficult to hold the committee to one or several well-defined positions. As President Porteus reiterated the theme that chairmen should strive for consensus committee decisions which could receive overwhelming convention support, this also influenced the manner in which the chairmen saw and played their respective roles.

To prepare the members of their committees for decision making and the drafting chores ahead, most chairmen initially invited expert witnesses to appear and discuss the general subjects within their jurisdiction. This lent legitimacy to the committee, furnished background knowledge for uninformed delegates, and aided independent initiation within the committee, countering the need otherwise to rely solely on the introduced printed proposal. Once the members were briefed on the ramifications of their responsibilities, attention was turned to the specific proposals before the committee. Heads of executive departments were invited to testify on matters pertinent to their agencies. Sometimes subcommittees reported on specific problems, or submitted drafts for full committee consideration. In the 1968 convention, since each committee had jurisdiction over all of one or more articles in the constitution, they did not feel constrained to limit themselves to the proposals referred to them and, *seriatim*, section by section, brought up for consideration and disposed of these portions of the constitution.

When preparing their reports to the convention the committees included a statement on the purpose of the delegate proposals considered, and the findings and reasons for the committee recommendations. Each report concluded with the committee's recommendations for convention action. The committee report also indicated whether the reported delegates' proposals had been incorporated into the committee proposal accompanying the report.

Once a committee proposal was reported to the floor the standing committee chairman assumed its management in the Committee of the Whole. Frequently he lined up speakers on both sides and the presiding officer respected the arrangement in recognizing the delegates seeking to speak. In a few cases chairmen took differing positions from their committees, supporting minority committee reports or introduced amendments; for the most part, chairmen submerged their individual preferences and loyally supported their committees' recommendations. Insofar as possible the chairmen sought to retain committee solidarity while the committee proposal was before the convention and might call repeated committee caucuses to enable members to agree on a position on amendments being proposed from the floor. With each standing committee's membership constituting over a quarter of the total convention, it was usually difficult to defeat a committee proposal when a near unanimous front was maintained.

In preparing committee proposals the 1968 convention widely used the Ramseyer method of indicating deleted material in brackets and underscoring new materials added. As necessary, the Committee on Style removed this "surplusage" so that the language read as it was to be finally adopted when that committee reported back to the convention. The Committee on Style also employed bracketing and underscoring in its reports to aid the delegates in identifying stylistic changes. When the language of a committee proposal was rephrased, particularly on technically complicated or politically sensitive matters, care was taken to consult the chairman of the standing committee concerned. Not infrequently his staff was also involved, and the Committee on Style might have recourse to outside consultants as well.

In the 1968 convention the Committee on Style attempted to make the constitution a document "generally read and understood by all of the people." To this end the committee sought to remove all old and archaic English terms and uncommonly used foreign and Latin phrases. Clarity of language and consistency with current usage were also goals. Reluctantly, it occasionally had to admit defeat: "Your Committee made an effort to state in English the Latin phrase 'mutatis mutandis,' but could find no English equivalent acceptable to lawyers." One cannot help but wonder whether the committee's concern for the "average reader" would have been as assiduously pursued if the committee chairman and vice chairman, and its chief assistant, had been attorneys.

Under the rules the Committee on Style had power to rearrange the provisions adopted under the various committee proposals to permit their presentation in proper order. In its final action under this authority, the Committee on Style included unamended as well as amended sections, in effect improving the style of the constitution and avoiding inaccuracies and repetitions. The committee proceeded on the premise that the voters would be called on to ratify the entire product of the convention, including all the last-minute corrective adjustments which it inserted into its final report. This, in fact, is what occurred.

One commentator on the 1950 scene noted that it was often evident that delegates were somewhat unfamiliar with the implications of the proposals or the topics under discussion before the committees. As the weeks wore on there was a marked change. The delegates' serious study resulted in improving the quality of committee discussions. Again, when the committee reports were before the entire membership, some delegates were unfamiliar with the issues and the debates suffered accordingly. In the Committee of the Whole, proposals underwent substantial modifications with numerous amendments offered and debate often sharp and protracted. On the whole, however, discussions were on a high plane and directed to basic issues.

In 1968, delegates brought more governmental experience to their convention chores. Although there was no lack of amendments made on the floor, and at times debate waxed long and loud, for the most part it was not of the same eloquence as that of the 1950 convention. In the earlier body there was more cutting and reworking of committee proposals, in part because the total picture was not apparent until the various provisions were brought together in the final form of a constitution. In 1968 the constitutional frame was established within which amendments were to be fitted, and this served somewhat as a damper on delegates whose actions might otherwise have inclined more to eccentric innovation.

The convention rules permitted a delegate during Committee of the Whole to propose amendments which had been previously defeated in the standing committee, and to offer them later on second reading in plenary session after they had been turned down in the Committee of the Whole. In 1968 this earned the ire of many delegates who wanted to move the convention along more rapidly. They complained that the procedure rendered the debates and votes in the Committee of the Whole meaningless. To counter this, 63 delegates introduced a resolution which proposed either to eliminate the Committee of the Whole or to preclude amendments to any proposal on second reading, except by two-thirds consent of the members present. President Porteus referred the resolution to the Rules Committee, and it languished there despite its apparently strong sponsorship. The explanation for this lies partially in the president's mollifying the objections of the dissatisfied delegates, in line with his commitment to an open convention with full opportunities for debate. The death of the resolution to amend the rules may also be attributed to the leadership of the chairman in keeping the measure bottled up in his committee. But, most satisfying as explanation, the sponsors had effectively shown their strength, a warning to the rest of the delegates not to persist in their attempts to resuscitate defeated amendments. Thereafter they did not find it necessary to make good their threat.

Leadership of the Presidents

The leadership of the presidents at both conventions was of singular importance. Externally they served well as spokesmen for their conventions, and the public respected them for this demonstration of competence. Within the convention their experience and good judgment aided them in guiding the delegates procedurally and, in a number of instances, substantively. President Porteus' tour with the 1950 convention, where his duties as secretary included oversight of the administrative, clerical and custodial staff, and also serving temporarily as vice chairman and presiding over the convention, provided him with a background that stood him in particularly good stead. This experience enabled him to have the conviction of his own views, and buttressed his introduction of procedural innovations on a number of occasions to aid the 1968 convention in overcoming restrictive technicalities. He had gone on record as favoring every delegate's right to have an opportunity to express his views and openly debate them, and he saw to it that the procedures of the 1968 convention observed those principles. Quietly, but firmly, he suggested solutions to problems raised by delegates and committees, settled jurisdictional difficulties when the concerned committee chairmen could not mutually resolve them, personally counseled delegates whose conduct he thought was unduly disturbing the course of convention business, bolstered weak chairmen by participating in their committees' deliberations, and watched over the work flow of the convention to see that it proceeded expeditiously. To delegates who had served under both presidents, King talked less and was a "faster man on the gavel." He also supplied more direction to the course of the convention, and more overtly pressed for rapid action. Porteus had to walk a diplomatic line between his promise of an open convention and the accommodation of the constant demand for a speedy conclusion to the convention's work, mainly by legislator-delegates.

One of the important contributions of the president was his working out a tentative time schedule of intermediate target dates with the other officers and the key committee chairmen, and then holding the convention resolutely to long hours as it pushed through to the final stages of debate. Cutoff points were established for the introduction of proposals in both conventions and, later, deadlines set for the submission of committee reports and their appended committee proposals. At the 1968 convention, in deference to the proposals that might originate from the Neighbor Islands as the delegates held hearings there, the final date for receipt of delegate proposals was fixed by the Rules Committee for three weeks after convening. The president made it understood, however, that all other proposals should be in a week earlier. Actually the deadline on delegate proposals was not too effective a device for placing a ceiling on the scope of the convention's activities. New matters could still be introduced through committee proposals and, in addition, both in Committee of the Whole and on second reading in general session, subjects could be initiated which had not been incorporated in any proposal.

Convention Sessions

Once over their initial organizing delays, four or five committees met each day so that, with attendance at plenary sessions and the studying of documents, delegates were called on to devote most of their time to constitutional tasks. Although the 1968 convention from the beginning held a pro forma general session each Saturday morning, neither convention made good use of that day until the tempo of work increased to a point when it was obvious the convention could no longer keep to a five-day week. Some of the Neighbor Island members returned home over the weekend, which resulted in Monday morning being poorly used, as well.

It was not until the twenty-eighth day of the 1950 convention that the delegates approved a six-day work week and a deadline for the submission of committee proposals was set. In 1950, all committees found it difficult to meet their assigned timing and, at first, a full week's extension was allowed, with which a bare majority of committees then managed to comply. The remainder encountered greater difficulty in submitting their final reports, and one committee received four extensions before its membership could agree and report on the proposals before it. At the 1968 convention it was apparent from the outset that districting and reapportioning the legislature would be the most time-consuming issues. The submission and consideration of other committee reports was, therefore, encouraged so they could be concluded before the convention turned to legislative mapping. By the time proposals were reported out by the various committees, and it was evident that long debate was in store for the delegates, sessions running from early morning to late at night, six days a week, became standard practice.

Both conventions suffered minor interruptions which interfered with the orderly course of convention work. To reassure the people on the Neighbor Islands that the convention was concerned with them and their problems, a series of meetings of the respective county delegations and a few key committee chairmen was held outside of Honolulu. This had only a minor parallel in the 1950 convention, where one public meeting was held on Lanai to discuss the possibility of that island becoming a separate county. No objections were raised to this inter-island travel, but the absence of the delegates on the mainland in both conventions drew public condemnation. In 1950, one-quarter of the convention, including all of the officers but the secretary, appeared at statehood hearings in Washington, which noticeably slowed down the work of the convention for a week. No comparable diminution of activity occurred at the 1968 convention when seven delegates were scheduled to attend their national party convention on the mainland. Nevertheless, it drew a petition of protest alleging that this constituted an abridgment of responsibility.

Citizen Interest in the Convention

During the course of both conventions, citizen interest was never great enough to encourage more than a handful of people to attend meetings. On occasion, public hearings of committees on controversial issues drew attendance of from 50 to a hundred persons. At regular committee meetings, few more members of the public than witnesses assembled, and the latter many times only at the request of the committee to appear and testify. Despite all the attention given to the selection of a site for the general sessions that could afford ample space for spectators, their absence was conspicuous. Occasionally a school teacher mustered her whole class in attendance. Other than for the opening day ceremonies, and the 1950 closing celebration, the convention lacked drawing appeal and the public stayed away. The same held true with regard to personal contacts between constituents and delegates. Except for the relatively small number of advocates who supported positions related to constitutional change, few members of the public in any way contacted their delegates to express their views on pending issues. Even the attempt of some delegates to bridge the communication gap by taking the initiative proved unrewarding. Two weeks after 8,000 letters were mailed to his constituents soliciting comments on constitutional content, one delegate had received only 15 replies and the rate of return did not materially increase thereafter.

As the one notable exception, at both conventions the League of Women Voters maintained close watch over convention deliberations. While still a provisional league in 1950, the organization sponsored study groups and discussion units in the city and county of Honolulu in order to keep its members and the public informed of convention activities. The observers at the 1968 convention similarly reported to the league's membership.

Perhaps accounting for the general lack of personal involvement on the part of the public was the breadth of mass media coverage, reporting all that went on in committee and on the convention floor. Besides the press, radio, and television in 1968, weekly releases were prepared by the Committee on Submission and Information which were widely distributed, primarily to community groups. At the 1950 convention the radio stations donated time each week for summaries of the work of the convention. In 1968 the educational TV channel carried many hours of convention debate live every day, a weekly review of convention happenings, and scheduled interviews with all of the committee chairmen. There was no lack of opportunity for the average citizen to be kept informed of what was occurring in the convention, so his failure to attend personally may not be attributed solely to apathy.

Party and Union Influence

Both in 1950 and in 1968, organized political party influence was not a major factor in directing the course of the conventions. Delegates had been chosen in nonpartisan elections, so there was no compelling need to carry over partisan politics to the convention floor. Aside from the occasional party reference, frequently to score debaters' points or introduce a humorous note, their role was sporadic and lacked a basis of pre-conceived strategy. In both conventions the majority party represented was able to obtain some advantage on the final apportionment agreed on for the legislature, but the Republican's gains in 1950 later appeared to backfire, and those which the Democrats sought on Oahu in 1968 may similarly prove not to fulfill their expectations.

In 1950 the unions were small, "arrogant"—the description used by one delegate to both conventions—and not a material force in decision making. By 1968, agricultural, industrial and governmental employee unions had become a major political power in the community, and at times their influence carried over to convention delegates beholden to them. The proposal favoring collective bargaining for governmental employees brought considerable union pressure to bear on the delegates and helped secure its adoption. Organized business groups, such as chambers of commerce, also made formal presentations and informally contacted delegates through such means as the time-honored practice of extending dinner invitations. In the main their lobbying activities were low-pitched and had relatively little effect on the decisions reached. The ad hoc bloc which attempted to sell the "merit plan" for the selection of state justices and judges was conspicuous not alone by the aggressiveness of its public "educational" campaign, but also by contrast with the very little use of mass public persuasion attempted by other pressure groups. Sometimes, "back-scratching" (reciprocal trading) helped line up delegates; occasionally, on crucial votes, delegates reported receipt of promises of support to their campaigns in the forthcoming elections, and even proffers of office in the next legislature, if only they would cast their ballot as requested. For the most part, delegates supported or opposed proposals on the basis of personal judgment, or the logic of other delegates when they did not have the conviction of their own.

Convention Workways and Cost

The constitutional convention in 1950 met on 79 working days over a 101-day span. The body which convened in 1968 tallied 57 working days within the 72-day period from convening until recessing for the printing of the revised constitution and its preparation for signature. Actually the 1968 convention never adjourned. After the signing ceremony the president continued to hold it in recess so as to remove any basis for technical objection to the convention's spending money thereafter in educating the public on the provisions to be put on the ballot.

In all the 1950 convention received 196 proposals from delegates and 31 committee proposals. In the first week alone of the 1968 constitutional convention, delegates introduced almost as many proposals (181) as the total of the whole previous convention. By the time the cutoff date had been reached, 325 delegate proposals had been presented—this for a constitution hailed as requiring no changes other than for legislative reapportionment and amendment of the debt ceiling. In both conventions, about the same number of resolutions was introduced: 56 in 1950, 51 in 1968. In view of the fact that a new constitution was being drafted in 1950, there was a relatively large number of committee proposals, the provisions of which were later rearranged and combined by the Committee on Style into the format of the present constitution. At the 1968 convention, now working within that format, it was possible for the committees to direct their reports to the entirety of a single constitutional article. As a result there were fewer committee proposals (13). Numbers qua numbers are misleading, though, as there were many duplicates of delegate proposals, and the length of a proposal can vary greatly with neither the complexity of the issue nor the work necessitated by committee and convention measured by the number of words. At the 1968 convention, one of the delegates introduced the whole of the state constitution, expressly making only a few changes, but implying thereby that he was willing to condone the various committees' considering the totality of the constitution should they be so inclined.

The sum of $250,000 was appropriated for the expense of the 1950 constitutional convention. Excluding the delegate's stipend and the cost of conducting both primary and runoff elections, it was estimated that less than $75,000 remained for running the convention. The appropriation had been premised on the assumption that the convention would complete its work in approximately 60 days, which proved ill-founded. Eventually it was necessary to request supplementary funds from the territorial governor. The convention received an extra $45,000. Throughout, the limited funds served as a constraining force, keeping the delegates mindful of the necessity to trim their demands narrowly. When they adjourned, their drafting chores completed, only $6,500 remained to conduct the post-election educational campaign.

For the 1968 convention, three times as much was provided for delegates' stipends, and over 13 times as much as originally appropriated in 1950. President Porteus, however, was not of a mind to spend all this money, and kept a firm control over it. To his critics, he was "out to make

a record" in support of future political aspirations. When some of the
delegates urged installation of air-conditioning in the McKinley gymnasium where the plenary sessions were held, he vetoed the suggestion on
the basis of cost. Delegates were denied the privilege of charging long-
distance messages to the convention telephone system without his or
the secretaries' express approval. Similarly, he limited the amount of
delegate travel to the Neighbor Islands, although it must be added that
this also negated any impression that these trips constituted junketing.
At the outset he announced his plan to return a surplus to the state
treasury and, when the convention books were closed, he had succeeded
to the extent that a third of the amount appropriated had not been spent.

CONVENTION COSTS

	1950	1968
Total Appropriation	$250,000[a]	$1,500,000[b]
Election Costs	114,100	295,000
Delegates' Compensation	63,000	205,000
Running Convention	72,900[c]	1,000,000
(Expended):		
Delegates' per diem	..	224,200
Employees' remuneration	76,900	345,900
Supplies, equipment, etc.	31,200	93,400
Surplus (deficit)	(35,200)[d]	336,500[e]

[a] Later supplemented by $45,000 from Governor's Contingency Fund.
[b] Does not include $100,000 for pre-convention educational program, nor extra
$80,000 to the Legislative Reference Bureau for convention services.
[c] As of 79th convention day, July 22, 1950.
[d] Additional $3,300 expended either for employees, supplies or both, subse-
quent to 79th day; with $45,000 supplement, $6,500 left for post-convention
citizen education.
[e] Surplus after expending $19,900 for post-convention advertising, and about
$20,000 in other expenses for citizen education.

It was a deliberate gamble to choose a site for holding the convention
which would have to be vacated if work were not completed with des-
patch, and it was lost. First, use of the Kapiolani Community College facilities and then the McKinley High School gymnasium—Convention Hall, itself—were denied. In contrast to the relative opulence which
marked the convening, as the initial acts of retrenchment, delegates'
offices and reserved parking places were surrendered and the staff was
drastically cut. Finally the delegates ignobly walked out of "Con-Con
Hall," carrying their wastepaper baskets into which they had crammed

personal files and work papers, and later crowded together in the Senate chamber of Iolani Palace to finish their task. Without the unifying force of statehood which had held the 1950 convention together and particularly gave meaning to the conclusion of its efforts, the 1968 convention turned more of its attention to looking at the trees in lieu of concern for the forest, and this lack of a unifying force became ever more manifest as the convention drew to a close. The impression left was one of winding down to a final halt, with the many delegates seeking elective public office breathing an obvious sigh of relief that they were now free to give full attention to this more pressing concern.

8.

The Convention Product

The 1950 constitution gave the Congress of the United States a preview of Hawaii the state. It showed and was meant to demonstrate how thoroughly the people of the Islands were imbued with American political and cultural traditions. The proposed constitution closely followed both the federal constitution, which it specifically adopted, and the requirements set forth in the statehood enabling legislation then pending before the Congress. The mandates of this bill prescribed that the constitution should embody the principles of religious freedom; nondiscrimination in civil or political rights because of race, color or sex; establishment and maintenance of a system of public schools open to all children and free from sectarian control; state assumption of territorial debts and liabilities; and taxation of nonresidents' property at no higher rate than that applied to property of Hawaiian residents. The Hawaiian Homes Commission Act also was to be incorporated and protected as state law, and the state was to accede to federal land holdings in the Islands. That the constitution must also be republican in form posited a less definite criterion than the others, for probably Congress would not have objected to the inclusion of a provision calling for the direct adoption of legislation if the drafters of the 1950 constitution and the voters had been of such a mind.

The proposals considered by the delegates to the 1950 convention encompassed not only all those provisions in the Organic Act possibly pertinent to state government, but also a wide range of other matters which proved attractive to the delegates, or at least to their constituents. The initiative, referendum and recall, although advocated actively by a small citizens' group organized for the purpose, received the support of few delegates. The unicameral legislature concept soon was rejected. A difficult fight over the sizes of the two legislative houses and their apportionment sharply divided the delegates. So did the determination of gubernatorial fiscal powers.

A large group of the Hawaiian population, concerned over the possibility of losing the protection of the Hawaiian Homes Commission, met in prayer to preserve this institution. The constitution as drafted assured the retention of the commission, and of land set aside for rehabilitation of persons of Hawaiian ancestry.

The final constitutional document guaranteed and protected all essential human rights under a comprehensive bill of rights. While the articles on the executive, legislative and judicial branches of government followed in large measure the traditional American pattern, they also contained some provisions deemed highly progressive: a broad grant of legislative power; automatic reapportionment of the lower house; appointment of judicial officers by the executive, subject to legislative approval; streamlining of the executive branch; adoption of a short ballot by limiting the elective executive posts to two, the governor and lieutenant governor; and specification for executive budgeting and a civil service system based on the merit principle. The voting age was reduced to 20, the age of majority in Hawaii. Persons in private employment were recognized to have the right to organize for the purpose of collective bargaining, and public employees the right to organize and to make their grievances known. Protection of public health and promotion of the public welfare were declared as objectives of government, as were conservation of land, resources and natural beauty. The document was commendably short, some 14,000 words, and represented the victory of those who held for sketching the structure of government, positing its powers in general language, and leaving out everything specific that was not essential by way of overcoming negative legal interpretations or protecting the rights of the people.

The convention had legal power to adopt ordinances to implement the constitution, which would require ratification by the people to become effective. It was contemplated that these would be transitional measures, to facilitate the transfer of government from the territory to the state. The 1950 convention never exercised this authority, in part because those provisions considered important were incorporated into the constitution, while it was believed preferable to leave the balance to the legislature as statutory in nature. On the basis of the experience with the first constitution, no comparable ordinance power was granted the 1968 convention.

Nine years later, as limitations or conditions to Hawaii's statehood, the voters expressed approval on four proposals raised by the United States Congress: (1) that Hawaii should be immediately admitted to the Union; (2) the state boundaries as fixed in the congressional act were accepted; (3) the rights reserved by the United States over lands in the state were agreed to; and (4) the provisions applying to the Hawaiian Homes Commission were amended to comply with language Congress desired in the state constitution. These became binding by virtue of the vote of the people, not the convention which drafted the constitution. Other amendments adopted since statehood had included provision for an elected board of education, joint ballot for governor and lieutenant governor, and minor modification in the membership of boards and in the boundaries of a legislative district as specified in the constitution's schedule. The original draft submitted to the voters in 1950, and the express and implied amendments since then, comprised the constitution reviewed by the delegates in 1968.

The delegates to the 1950 convention had almost free reign in expressing their philosophy of government in the language of the proposed state constitution. Not so the delegates of 1968, who now had presented to them a complete blueprint for the structure of the functioning state polity, and faced the undertaking of a program for action in part mandated by the federal courts. The product which emerged from the 1968 deliberations consequently could be expected to be more confirmatory than novel, more amendatory than revolutionary, and more concerned with the details of implementation than the broad sweep of philosophic formulation.

The delegates, by virtue of the form of the ballot they gave to the voters, divided the proposed amendments into 23 "highlights." In some instances a single highlight encompassed a number of disparate and only distantly related matters, in short, a catchall for miscellany. For the most part, however, each of the highlights was either the single or central issue, the other conjoined amendments becoming appurtenances. The ballot format thus nicely lends itself to identification of the product of the 1968 constitutional convention.

THE HIGHLIGHTS

1. Apportionment and Districting of Legislature

During the territorial period, Hawaii remained unreapportioned for 50 years, this despite the mandate of the Organic Act for redistricting every decade on the basis of territorial citizenship. The 1950 constitution proposed to break the impasse by using registered voters as the apportionment base, thereby eliminating the excuse that territorial citizenship data was unavailable. When Hawaii's apportionment was challenged before the United States Supreme Court, the use of registered voters was upheld in that body's decision, just so long as it did not materially deviate from a permissible population base. Confronting the 1968 convention was the knowledge that the distribution of registered voters did not correspond with that of the population, in part because Hawaii's peoples have long continued to vote illegally from precincts where they no longer reside, not bothering to change their registration. Also looming importantly, sizable blocs of the population are not eligible to register.

Total population as an apportionment base carried the disability of including large pockets of military and maritime personnel on Oahu, which constitute appreciable proportions of the total population within their legislative districts. Violent fluctuations in their numbers, which have occurred in the past, would substantially distort relative representative ratios from year to year. In addition, since the official census is taken decennially, it was believed that it could not truly reflect Hawaii's rapidly changing population, just as the 1960 census was out of date for the 1968 reapportionment computations, and that in all likelihood this would cause a further deviation from equality of population among the districts. Total population as a basis was therefore abandoned.

Permanent population, which by definition excludes transient and nonresident elements, proved to be unworkable because data on the place of residence of the military personnel and their dependents is not available.

Civilian population could not be adopted as an appropriate base for apportionment because military personnel would be arbitrarily excluded. Under the rule of *Davis* v. *Mann,* such an exclusion would be constitutionally prohibited. In any event, even if constitutionally permissible, the standing committee stressed that it would not utilize this base. Its concern over the inclusion of the military ran not against military personnel, per se, but rested entirely on the impact of their fluctuating numbers on state population estimates necessary to determine districting.

Citizen population at first appeared a feasible basis. When it was realized that it is not possible to obtain statistics concerning the residence of aliens with sufficient detail to permit the drawing of legislative district boundaries, this, too, was abandoned as suffering the same shortcomings as both total population and permanent population.

Like the others, *eligible voter population* carried its own disadvantages. Estimates could be calculated from each decennial federal census for the apportionment and reapportionment of legislative districts, but within five years thereafter the data would become very inadequate. As proof of this, reference was made to the published statistic of 112.3 percent of the extrapolated eligible voter population in Kauai County having voted in 1966, "an obvious impossible ratio."

By a process of elimination, and as a logical extension of the eligible voter base, the 1968 convention settled on *registered voters* for the apportionment of districts. Through the report of its standing committee, the convention laid the groundwork for justifying its continuation of the registered voter base. The strong involvement of Hawaii's citizens in politics, the high rate of voter turnout, and the active role of election personnel in encouraging registration, together with Hawaii's continuous registration law, were all cited as supporting the use of this base. Probably the most telling reason of all was the desire to have more frequent than decennial reapportionment, and the ready fit of registration statistics for achieving this purpose. Finally, anticipating court challenge, express provision was incorporated into the constitution directing that the legislature provide a chief election officer of the state, one of whose duties would be to maximize eligible voter registration and maintain data to facilitate reapportionment.

Once having decided on continuing the use of the registered voter base, the delegates had no recourse but to rely on 1966 registration data. Current lists of electors would remain open until the primary elections in October 1968, long after the convention was to be concluded. The 1968 constitutional convention election data were suspect in that they were compiled for a special election and may not have equitably represented the registration distribution occurring at a normal, general election. As a practical matter, if the convention did not utilize the 1960 census data, or some derivative thereof, of necessity it had to turn to the 1966 registration statistics.

Just as in 1950, in 1968 the subject of legislative apportionment and, more specifically, how the lines of the representative and senatorial districts were to be drawn, held the central attention of the delegates. Just as in 1950, the standing committee charged with legislative apportionment and districting in 1968 found it "impossible to reapportion or redistrict the state without jeopardizing the ability of some of the incumbent state legislators (as well as of some prospective candidates who are not incumbents) to gain reelection." The committee could also have added that the increase in size of Oahu's population relative to the Neighbor Islands made it difficult to retain incumbent legislators from districts outside of Honolulu. The 1950 convention resolved the latter problem by expanding the size of the two houses (Senate from 15 to 25 and House of Representatives from 30 to 51) but in 1968 the majority of the delegates was content to retain the legislative bodies unaltered, and, if necessary, to countenance the non-return of incumbents whose districts might be eliminated. The convention found some comfort in the legal fact that residence requirements for legislative candidacy are prescribed by statute and not by the constitution. It recommended to future legislatures that they temporarily waive residence requirements for candidates whose districts have been altered by reapportionment.

Next, using the method of equal proportions, the membership of the Senate and the House of Representatives was divided among the four basic island units—Kauai, Niihau; Maui, Molokai, Lanai; Hawaii; Oahu— the last including any other area not encompassed elsewhere. This apportionment was in line with the committee's recommendation that each basic island unit be guaranteed a minimum representation. In this, the 1968 convention was concurring with the earlier body in attempting,

Basic Island Units—House of Representatives

Island Unit	No. of Reps.	No. of Reg. Voters[a]	Reg. Voters per Rep.	% Dev. from State Aver. of 4,966[b]
Hawaii	6	28,596	4,766	− 4.0
Maui	4	19,029	4,757	− 4.2
Oahu	38	193,107	5,082	+ 2.3
Kauai	3	12,510	4,170	−16.0
Total/Avg.	51	253,242	4,966	0.0

[a] Based on the 1966 General Election Voters List (before purge).
[b] Total statewide number of registered voters divided by the total number of representatives.

Basic Island Units—Senate

Island Unit	No. of Sen.	No. of Reg. Voters[a]	Reg. Voters per Senator	% Dev. from State Aver. of 10,130[b]
Hawaii	3	28,596	9,532	− 5.9
Maui	2	19,029	9,515	− 6.1
Oahu	19	193,107	10,164	+ 0.3
Kauai	1	12,510	12,510	+23.5
Total/Avg.	25	253,242	10,130	0.0

[a] Based on the 1966 General Election Voters List (before purge).
[b] Total statewide number of registered voters divided by the total number of senators.

insofar as possible, to preserve the integrity of Hawaii's historical units. Indeed, as to be explained, through providing for fractional representation the delegates in 1968 went farther than even the 1950 convention had dared.

The basic island unit of Kauai's disproportionate representation in the two houses is due to the fact that its population approximates neither one nor a multiple number of the state's average unit of population used as the basis for apportionment. Despite the wide percentage deviations, the convention believed that Kauai's overrepresentation in the House of Representatives (—16.0 percent) to a large extent would compensate for the underrepresentation in the Senate (+23.5 percent), under the doctrine of *Reynolds* v. *Sims*. In that case the Supreme Court had indicated that apportionment in one house (of a bicameral legislature) could be arranged so as to balance off minor inequities in the representation of certain areas in the other house.

Once the Committee on Legislative Apportionment and Districting decided to recommend that the existing size of both houses be retained, major attention turned to reconstituting the House of Representatives. The temporary apportionment plan for the Senate which was approved by the Supreme Court in *Burns* v. *Richardson* allocated 19 senators to Oahu, three to Hawaii, two to Maui and one to Kauai. This apportionment could remain undisturbed, as it roughly approximated the distribution of current registered voters, in contrast to the inadequacy of the apportionment of the House. No delegate was of a mind to open up the subject of Senate apportionment, principally because no dissatisfaction was expressed with the functioning of the temporary plan. As a consequence the 1968 convention concurred in its committee's conclusion ". . . that the Senate districting plan now temporarily in effect under the ruling of *Burns* v. *Richardson* . . . is sound and acceptable, with some minor adjustments of boundary lines of two urban Oahu districts."

One of the issues of the campaign concerned the size of legislative districts. The International Longshoremen's and Warehousemen's Union strongly advocated single-member districts, at least for one house. To assist the Committee on Legislative Apportionment and Districting in tackling this issue, through computer processing of census and registration data for Oahu, two separate apportionment plans were prepared reflecting all single-member districts, and at least five plans containing only multi-member districts. Confronted with the results, the committee concluded that it could not recommend to the convention any plan which was limited rigidly to single- or multi-membered districts. Reasons for rejecting only single-member districts were that such a system: (a) unduly disrupts and divides areas where people have a substantial community of interest; (b) results in irrational district lines; and (c) is subject to violent shifts in district boundary lines at each apportionment, especially where the population is changing rapidly. Such violent shifts in district lines detract from the stability desired in Hawaii's political process. On the other hand, proposals for all multi-member districts were rejected because: (a) areas which are substantially homogeneous in the socioecenomic makeup of their population, and distinctly different from that of the people in the adjoining areas, if sufficiently large and geographically separable ought to be representative districts by themselves; and (b) single-member districts should be utilized for sparsely populated areas. The ILWU's representatives and all others previously advocating single-member districts for one house of the legislature were convinced by the demonstration, as buttressed by the committee's logic, and the issue disappeared from further convention concern.

In selecting a districting plan, the committee adopted a set of criteria which could also serve as guidelines for future reapportionment:

1) The average number of . . . voters per legislator in every district shall be as nearly equal as possible. (As a restatement of the equal population principle enunciated by the United States Supreme Court, this criterion was given overriding consideration.)

2) No district shall extend beyond county boundaries.

3) Insofar as possible, districts are to be contiguous (except multi-island districts) and compact.

4) District lines must follow permanent and easily recognized lines—e.g., major streets, streams, clear geographical features—and should follow census tract lines where possible.

5) Wherever possible, the division of areas with a substantial community of interest (socioeconomic) is to be avoided.

6) The submersion of small areas or groups within larger districts where substantially different socioeconomic interests predominate is to be avoided. . . . Where a socioeconomic group of people cannot, by reason of its number or otherwise, be a district by itself, it should have at least a fighting chance to compete with other socioeconomic groups in the same district in selecting a legislator.

7) Districts may not be so drawn as to unduly favor one person or political faction.

8) No multi-member House district shall have more than three Representatives. (This criterion, however, premised on the desire to enable voters to become acquainted with their candidates, was relaxed for future reapportionments, where a maximum of four Representatives per district is countenanced.)

9) No single-member districts shall be created in highly urban areas. (While the committee found that no rational single-member district lines could now be drawn in any of Hawaii's urban areas, this criterion was not adopted for future reapportionment when data then existing might justify single-member districts.)

10) Except where districts constitute entire islands or counties, the Senate districts should be larger than Representative districts, and Senate district lines should avoid cutting across a House district.

In seeking to reduce the disparity in district size to a minimum, the committee followed the working rule that no deviation from the average number of registered voters per legislator should exceed 10 percent, except in unusual circumstances to be explicitly explained. Wherever possible, deviations were to be held to within 5 percent.

Upon facing the difficult task of delineating the districts, some disagreements occurred over exactly where to run the lines and the number of legislators to be assigned to each district. Abstract principles are sometimes easier to agree on than specifics which may spell the election or defeat of a particular politician. In 1950 the convention adopted the alternative of generally running the boundaries of legislative districts from the mountains to the sea, following the concept of the old Hawaiian *ahupua'a*. The redistricting completed and the constitution adopted by the voters, it was claimed that on Oahu this configuration was designed to aid the Republicans. In truth, it ought to be added that the first election under this 1950 reapportionment saw the Democrats obtaining augmented strength in the legislative halls.

In 1968, 39 separate House districting plans were considered, 22 for the island unit of Oahu, 10 for Hawaii, three for Maui, and four for Kauai. In general the principle of representative district lines running from the mountains to the sea continued to be honored, but for the "city" of Honolulu, the urbanized area on the leeward side of Oahu, existing districts were split into smaller units mainly by using the course of the new freeways. These automobile throughways were treated as both physically and psychologically dividing the neighborhoods through which they run, frequently demarking socioeconomic cleavages. In addition, the freeways were originally sited in good part without regard to legislative incumbents, potential candidates or political parties, so in themselves they embodied the appearance of impartiality. The constitution of 1950 recognized the district's radial character; the constitution of 1968 added a new bisecting element which, for the "city" of Honolulu at least, probably presages future revamping which will draw even farther away from the traditional districting of old Hawaii.

SENATORIAL AND REPRESENTATIVE DISTRICTING

	Senatorial		Representatives			Reg. Voters Per Sen.[a]	Reg. Voters Per Rep.[a]	% Dev. per Sen.[b]	% Dev. per Rep.[c]
	Dist.	No.	Dist.	No.					
Hawaii	1	3	1	1		9,532	4,377	−5.9	−11.9
			2	2			5,058		+1.9
			3	1			4,766		−4.0
			4	1			4,517		−9.0
			5	1			4,821		−2.9
Maui	2	2	6	2		9,515	4,612	−6.1	−7.1
			7	2			4,903		−1.3
Oahu	3	3	23	3		10,018	4,702	−1.1	−5.3
			24	3			5,316		+7.1
			19	2			5,267		+6.1
	4	4	20	3		10,092	4,937	−0.4	−0.6
			21	1			5,725		+15.3
			22	2			4,648		−6.4
	5	4	15	2		10,276	5,252	+1.4	+5.8
			16	2			5,550		+11.8
			17	2			4,569		−8.0
			18	2			5,182		+4.3
	6	4	12	3		10,175	4,983	+0.4	+0.4
			13	3			5,199		+4.7
			14	2			5,078		+2.3
	7	4	8	2		10,221	5,225	+0.9	+5.2
			9	2			4,987		+0.4
			10	2			5,225		+5.2
			11	2			5,006		+0.8
Kauai	8	1[d]	25	3		12,510	4,170	+23.5	−16.0

[a] Based on the 1966 General Election Voters List (before purge).
[b] Deviation from statewide average per senator.
[c] Deviation from statewide average per representative.
[d] As Kauai was supposed to have two senators each with one-half vote, shown as 1.

When the committee had concluded its work, half of the 25 representative districts (13) were within a 5 percent deviation from the statewide average for the number of registered voters per representative, and all but four fell within the less than 10 percent maximum. Except for the 8th senatorial district on Kauai, all senatorial districts were well within the 10 percent deviation from statewide average number of registered voters per senator.

In all cases the convention justified these major deviations. Kauai's population did not lend itself to any other treatment, unless it is to be combined with another county. On Oahu, two atypical districts reflect an attempt to observe the criterion of keeping homogeneous areas intact wherever possible. On Hawaii, due to topography, dispersal of population and vast size, it was alleged to be impossible to narrow the deviation after taking into account the various demographic features. For the most part, districts were kept close to the state median; the former big House districts on Oahu, however, were broken up into smaller, more homogeneous units, while the larger and heterogeneous Senate districts accommodated a wider range of social, economic and political factors.

Not all of the delegates were satisfied with the redistricting as proposed by the committee. The chairman had anticipated this, and through persuasion and consensus had minimized internal dissention and built a strong committee solidarity. This loyalty crossed political party lines and committee members held firm even though floor amendments might be to their party's advantage. When necessary, due to the logic and size of the opposition, the committee agreed to compromise. Consequently, dissenters were able to secure adjustments in the Committee of the Whole in only a few cases. The delegates adopted the philosophy of their standing committee, and went along almost entirely with its recommendations on district boundaries.

If the new representative and senatorial districts are combined, so that the total representation in both houses for the population of any one senatorial district is computed, the number of registered voters per legislator in each combined district deviates from the statewide average by no more than 11.5 percent. Indeed, in all but one of the combined districts (Oahu 7th senatorial), this deviation was kept under 6.1 percent. The net effect of this reapportionment over the accomplishments of the 1950 constitutional convention was to redistrict the state to bring the effective ratio of representation closer to the one man, one vote principle enunciated by the United States Supreme Court. Whether it is close enough to obtain a favorable ruling by the federal courts remains to be tested.

2. Provision for Future Reapportionment

As an aid to orderly reapportionment the convention abandoned the staggering of senators' terms. Those elected in November 1968 were to serve only two years; starting in 1970, and every fourth year thereafter, all 25 senators will be elected for four years. The justification was that this would permit frequent reapportionment (every eight years) without the concommitant embarrassment of arbitrarily assigning incumbents to newly drawn districts, thus facilitating the work of a reapportionment commission, another innovation proposed by the 1968 convention.

The constitution drawn in 1950 made no provision for reapportionment of the Senate, a feature which was later stricken as unconstitutional. As for the House of Representatives, the governor was to reapportion and, if necessary, redistrict that body every 10 years, but only when the average of registered voters per representative in a district varied by more than 50 percent from the state average, and then the lines were to be redrawn so that the variation would be reduced to less than 50 percent. Given the extensive use of multi-member districts in the state, the governor's redistricting power was limited. With unexplained deviations of less than 12 percent being found unconstitutional in other jurisdictions, the validity of this provision in the original constitution was suspect. Further complicating the picture, the state legislature, in its attempt to adopt a stopgap provision for reapportionment of the Senate in 1965, had included in its proposed amendment language similar to that already in the constitution with relation to the House on the 50 percent variation. The delegates to the 1968 constitutional convention would have none of this.

In an attempt to reduce deviations to "an absolute minimum unless carefully and legally acceptable explanations for specific exceptions are made" and "because . . . Hawaii's very rapid growth in mobile population . . . will necessarily require redistricting which may be extensive [in all future reapportionments]" the convention looked favorably on incorporating into the constitution provision for an administrative districting agency. The standing committee chose from mainland state provisions those features which it considered most likely to be effective and improvised others specifically designed for Hawaii.

An ad hoc commission of nine members is to be established for each reapportionment, composed of eight members selected, equally, by the majority and minority parties of each house, and a ninth co-opted by the eight legislative designees. In addition the reapportionment commission will be assisted by advisory councils from the four legislative island units.

Legislators are not declared ineligible for membership on the reapportionment commission. Incumbents are effectively barred, however, unless they plan to retire, by the prohibition against anyone serving on the commission or the advisory councils becoming a candidate for legislative office for the next two elections under any reapportionment plan he prepares.

The first commission will serve in 1973, and a new one every subsequent eighth year. This has the effect of making the reapportionment ordered by the 1968 convention, and approved by the voters, effective only for the 1970 and 1972 elections.

3. Minimum Representation for Neighbor Islands

In recent years Oahu's population has grown at the relative and sometimes at the absolute expense of all the Neighbor Island counties. The constitutional convention devised a means to safeguard them against the ever-mounting concentration of legislative representation on Oahu should this trend not be reversed. While claiming not to "take issue with the basic philosophy underlying the one man, one vote principle," in effect the convention moved to overcome its practical impact. First, reference was made to Hawaii's geographical structure, with counties separated by large spans of open ocean, and to its simplified and centralized government, with more decisions made at the state capitol in Honolulu than would be true of mainland states with their more highly developed structures of local government. These, it was decided, were good and sufficient reasons for reassuring the Neighbor Island counties (in constitutional language technically referred to as "basic island units") of "effective representation" to cover legislative committee hearings, contact executive offices, and otherwise watch after their area's interests. Given the number of committees in the Senate and the House of Representatives, it was declared that a minimum of two senators and three representatives per unit is essential for "effective representation." When the population of the Neighbor Islands vis-à-vis Oahu does not support this minimum representation, fractional voting by their legislators is provided for. At the outset the county of Kauai beginning in 1970 was to have two senators, each with half a vote; at the reapportionment in 1973, or later, voting of other delegations could be fractionated.

There was grave question whether the provision for fractional voting would meet the constitutional test of equal representation when challenged before the courts. Granted that, in a roll call in the Senate, a basic island unit represented by two senators, each having one-half vote, would technically enjoy no greater voting strength than comparable representation by a single senator with a full vote. Nevertheless, in committees and in the informal legislative structure, half a vote may be sufficient to move or reject proposed legislation being screened or bargained on by the committee. Since each senator and representative, notwithstanding his partial vote, would also be entitled to all rights and privileges of his office, including full pay and allowances, the courts could easily conclude that this novel provision in Hawaii's constitution runs contrary to the spirit of equal representation. The convention delegates were skeptical of this part of their handiwork, and phrased the proposal in such a way that if it were to be held unconstitutional no further reapportionment or constitutional activity would be necessary. Their foresight was well-grounded, for "effective representation" was invalidated in its first court test. As a separable provision, fractional voting would merely drop out of the constitution.

4. Invasions of Privacy

In the endeavor to protect the individual's privacy as a matter of legitimate social interest, a declaration of the right to be secure in one's person, house, papers and effects against invasion of privacy is expressly written into the Bill of Rights. In addition, while recognizing that a warrant may be issued that might intercept a communication, protection is afforded by the requirement that the request for the warrant must be supported by a particular description. Undoubtedly some delegates considered this amendment as applicable principally to wiretapping; it will have a far broader impact, however, for it does not just encompass communications, but also establishes a new right to privacy in the state.

5. Dispensing with Bail

Currently, state courts in Hawaii waive bail if they are satisfied that a defendant charged with a criminal offense or a key witness will appear in court when directed. The constitutional change serves to ratify existing practices, removing doubts as to the discretionary powers of the court. Expressly excepted are defendants charged with offenses punishable by life imprisonment.

6. Counsel for Indigents Charged with Criminal Offenses

The United States Supreme Court's decision that indigent defendants must be offered the assignment of counsel in state courts when they are accused of serious crimes (*Gideon* v. *Wainwright*, 1963), led in a logical line of progression to the amendment of Hawaii's constitution in 1968 requiring the state to provide counsel for all indigent defendants charged with offenses punishable by imprisonment for more than 60 days. To the 1968 delegates the possibility of two months' imprisonment was sufficiently serious to require the attendance of counsel. It also was consonant with the thrust of more recent federal cases requiring an accused to be informed that he has the right to counsel before the police can interrogate him, and holding an accused has the right to counsel at a police "line up" and at hearings considering the revocation of parole.

7. Condemnation of Private Property

In the 1950 constitutional convention the Committee on Bill of Rights considered and rejected a proposal that the constitution mandate just compensation for the damaging of private property for public use when no actual "taking" occurs, as when a steep highway embankment is built so close to a house as to overshadow it and cause it to materially lose value. The prohibition against taking without compensation was retained, but the uncertainty of the term "damage" mitigated against inclusion of that provision. In 1968 the delegates impliedly concluded that the 1950 convention was too cautious. Precedents set in the 26 states whose constitutions mandate compensation for public "damage" were felt to provide workable guidelines for Hawaii under such a constitutional protection. As in the amendment to the Bill of Rights expressly recognizing the right of privacy, the scope of this new protection against damage without just compensation awaits delineation by Hawaii's courts.

As a footnote, the addition to the constitution of the phrase "damaged for public use" appeared awkward to the Committee on Style. But since "the language [was] designedly adopted from other jurisdictions, the body of law from which can provide guidelines in the legal interpretation of such words," the committee left the language completely unmodified. When meaning is ambiguous and interpretive assistance must be sought from any source, a style committee dare not flex its functions.

8. Reduction of Voting Age to 18 Years

Prior to the convening of the constitutional convention, the proposal that Hawaii's minimum voting age be lowered to 18 years (from 20) had drawn loud objection. Candidates reported encountering strong opposition in their constituencies, and some who had originally planned to campaign in favor of the proposal changed their strategies before the voters went to the polls. Nevertheless, lowering of the voting age carried the day at the convention. Possibly prophetically, the convention's youngest member—20 years old—opposed this expansion of the franchise.

In 1950 the Committee on Suffrage and Elections rejected 18 as the voting age on the ground that a person was "not politically mature at this age and two years will bring the necessary interest and understanding of the political life of Hawaii." In 1968 the convention respectfully disagreed, finding that 18-year-olds are politically mature enough to exercise the voting privilege responsibly. "With the passage of time and the change in our social environment and culture, the growing arguments for the eighteen-year-old vote have become increasingly convincing," declared the majority of the 1968 convention's Committee on Bill of Rights, Suffrage and Election. Six members dissented, holding for majority as the voting age and leaving the former to legislative determination. As Hawaii's age of majority currently is 20 years, this would in effect have retained the same minimum age for voting as now set in the constitution and transferred to the legislature full discretion to modify it either upwards or downwards.

Interest in the minimum voting age remained high, both in the community and on the convention floor. Attempts to beat down the standing committee's recommended reduction to 18 were unsuccessful in the convention, but the voters had the final say on the issue. When the ballots were tallied this was the only issue to be defeated at the polls! The distrust of youth and its suspected radicalism, which had manifested itself prior to the election of delegates, had carried over to the vote on the adoption of the convention's handiwork.

The 1967 session of the state legislature adopted a constitutional amendment proposing to grant 18-year-olds the vote. Since the requisite 10-day notice was not communicated to the governor prior to adoption, under the language of Hawaii's constitution it had to carry over for passage at a second session before being placed on the ballot. The constitutional convention then intervened. The 1969 legislators proved undaunted by the negative voter reaction to the issue and proposed a constitutional amendment to be placed on the ballot in 1970; the voters rejected it. The final outcome of the issue is likely to be affected by recent U. S. Supreme Court rulings upholding the 18-year-old vote for federal elections. Once again the state legislature is proposing to put the amendment on the state ballot, this time to save the extra costs now raised by allowing 18-year-olds to have only limited suffrage.

9. Voting Rights of Felons

The philosophy of expanding the franchise was not limited to minors, but also extended to felons and to the illiterate. Coupled with other recommended changes, as lowering the age required of legislative candidates and reducing the length of residence for executive officers, the convention disclosed an underlying consistency in attempting to broaden the scope of permissible political activity.

Like many states, Hawaii's constitution denied voting rights to felons until pardoned or restored to their civil rights. This the delegates were disposed to change, consistent with the endeavor to rehabilitate the felon and stimulate his sense of responsibility as a member of the community. The appropriate terminology proved difficult to phrase, due to the wide variety of circumstances under which persons convicted of felony may be released from physical incarceration but still be subject to constraints. As a compromise, "final discharge" was adopted as identifying the point of time at which the felon should once again be afforded the citizen's privilege to vote. In addition the legislature is empowered to recognize an earlier removal of the felon's disqualification, this to accommodate changing social mores and administrative conditions pertaining to felons.

10. Literacy as a Voting Requirement

As part of the Hawaiian heritage, ability to speak, read and write Hawaiian or English was established as a qualification to voting under the Territorial Organic Act. It was continued under the state constitution of 1950. Because it had become surplusage to a considerable extent, and because in spirit it was inconsistent with the federal Voting Rights Act of 1965, the 1968 convention proposed that the literacy requirement be entirely removed. At the ensuing election the voters concurred. What distinguishes this as unusual is that, just four years previously, a constitutional amendment proposed by the legislature to repeal this disfranchising provision had been defeated by a vote of 72,529 to 79,211, and nearly 63,000 people who went to the polls did not bother to vote on the issue.

11. Presidential Preference Primary

In at least one instance the 1968 convention labored mightily and produced relatively little for its efforts. On the recommendation of the Committee on Bill of Rights, Suffrage and Elections, the Committee of the Whole adopted a proposal directing the legislature to provide for a presidential preference primary. The dates and the exact form it was to take were to be left to the discretion of the legislature. In plenary session the delegates first concurred in the committee's recommendation but later eliminated the mandatory feature. As a consequence the legislature was expressly authorized to do what it has long had the inherent power to perform.

This left the informed voter, who desired a stronger direction, in something of a quandary. To vote against this innocuous provision could be interpreted by a hostile legislature as indicating popular disapproval of any presidential primary which, of course, would be the intent of an unsophisticated voter in casting a negative ballot. A majority of voters, for mixed motives, went along with the gentle nudge to modify Hawaii's practices for nominating a President, implicit in the incorporation of the explicit presidential primary authorization.

Possibly balancing this minimal effort at strengthening political party participation, an attempt was beaten down at the convention to eliminate Hawaii's closed primary law. Hawaii was long one of the few jurisdictions which allowed its voters full discretion to select among the candidates offered by all competing parties at primary elections. Gradually, in incremental steps, this has been curtailed, and starting with the election of 1970 a fully closed primary law became operative. Under the claim that secrecy of voting, as guaranteed by the constitution, encompasses secrecy of political party affiliation, an attempt was made to scuttle the law by prohibiting maintenance of a record of the party ballot selected by any voter. Delegates concluded that the proposed amendment was a matter for legislative determination and voted it down.

12. Minimum Age of Legislators

The minimum age for service as a member of either house of Hawaii's legislature has been one of the most restrictive in the United States. The ages of 30 for the upper house and 25 for the lower predated even the Organic Act and were imposed during the period of Hawaii's Republic. Their antecedents can be traced back to the United States constitution. With Hawaii being the "youngest" state, with its population recording a lower median age than the nation's, it would have been somewhat anachronistic if the 1968 convention had not questioned this requirement. The Committee on Legislative Powers and Functions would have retained this portion of the constitution unchanged, equating age's greater opportunity for involvement with a sense of community and social responsibility, and similarly identifying maturity and experience of age with capacity for careful weighing of conflicting interests and arguments, and all impliedly measured by the minimum age set forth in the 1950 constitution. Seven members of the committee demurred and filed a strong minority report. It was this position which carried the day, and the convention of 1968 accepted the committee's recommendation that the age of majority be the minimum age for legislators in either house. Somewhat ironically, while legal adulthood was felt to measure more closely one's capacity for undertaking community and social responsibilities than the age requirements previously set in the constitution, it was believed by the delegates to be too high for establishing the minimum age to vote. The voters felt otherwise and in effect related the two; it is now possible in Hawaii for a person reaching 20 years of age to both vote in his first election and, when doing so, cast a vote for himself as candidate for legislative office.

13. Legislative Detail

While it is the mode in modern constitution writing to eschew detail, preferring the use of the broad brush for sketching constitutional policy, an exception is ordinarily recognized in the case of provision made for the legislature. Baldly put, the average legislator does not—possibly cannot—keep himself and the procedures his house observes in line with the demands of the times. As a consequence, state constitutions prescribe a range of structure and procedure, a plethora of mandatory duties and prohibitions, which would be decried as unnecessary if applied to the executive or judicial branches. Hawaii is no exception, and the structures and procedures of the legislature were again tinkered with at the 1968 convention.

With regard to structure, the convention early and very quickly disposed of unicameralism by an advisory vote, opting for bicameralism in a vote of 66 to 10, with 6 delegates excused. In the absence of either scandal or exigency causing public disfavor with bicameralism, and lacking strong leadership sufficient to carry unicameralism through the barrier of inertia and against the drag of precedent, unicameralism for state legislatures is foredoomed. Once again, this time in Hawaii, the mock battle against bicameralism was fought and unicameralism appeared to make no greater advances than when it was proposed in 1950. The only difficulty the issue raised was procedural: how to dispose of it in advance so that the two legislative committees could get on with their work, safe in the knowledge that Hawaii's legislature would remain conventionally bicameral.

With so many members of the convention having legislative experience, they could understand the thermidor effect of the closing days of the legislative session, particularly the inability to study the compromise amendments made in free conference as the session draws to a close. To guarantee a minimum time for review, they included the mandate that 24 hours elapse between distribution of a bill in final form and its passage. This will not eliminate the logjam of measures, but it will at least help to mitigate some of the deleterious effects flowing from conference committee compromises being rammed through the legislature without the average legislator being aware of what he is voting on.

There was strong sentiment for annual sessions in the 1950 convention. Probably because of the amorphous public attitude that "no legislature is a good legislature," the compromise was adopted of interspersing a 30-day budget session in alternate years between the 60-day regular session. In 1968 the same desire to extend the working period of the legislature was reasserted, and this time it was successful by means both overt and covert. Overtly, the limited budget session is now replaced by a regular annual session, so that the distinction between the two forms has been erased, along with the artificial restrictions of the budget session. The delegates knew that the 1950 constitutional requirement that a measure be of urgent nature for it to receive budget-session consideration had been honored more in the breach than in the observance, simply by marshaling sufficient votes to label any measure "urgent." Covertly, the 1968 convention achieved a longer annual work period for the legislature by excluding from the 60-day limitation not only Sundays and holidays, which had not been computed under the 1950 constitution, but also Saturdays and "any day in recess pursuant to concurrent resolution." This assures at least a one-sixth increase on the permissible length of the regular session and will encourage the practice of long legislative recesses to facilitate committee work, probably stretching each session out through a good part of the calendar year.

From the inauguration of territorial status, the governor has enjoyed the discretion of extending regular and special sessions of the legislature for not more than 30 days. This power was continued by the state constitution. At the 1968 convention the period for permissible gubernatorial extension was halved, while the legislature, as an augmentation of its own status, was granted the power by an extraordinary two-thirds majority vote to extend its own life for up to 15 days. In addition, by comparable action it now may call itself into special session without gubernatorial sanction.

A number of minor adjustments accompanied the foregoing modifications. To make sure that the budget would be adopted in sufficient time before the commencement of the fiscal year on July 1, the date for convening each regular session was advanced by a full month. With the prospect that the legislative session might in effect continue throughout the year, express constitutional authorization was provided for carrying over a bill introduced at a session in an odd-numbered year to the next regular session, the practice observed by Congress. But, mindful of the caution against allowing abuse of the legislature's own prerogatives, any such measure must receive at least one reading in the house of origin before final adoption, this guarding against a bill being hurriedly enacted in the opening days of the second session.

14. Legislative Compensation

Both in 1950 and 1968 the convention was of the opinion that Hawaii's legislators should receive higher compensation. The 1950 convention granted the legislature the power to fix its own salary; recognizing that this was politically difficult, it included as an initial rate what was then the high salary of $2,500 for each general session, $1,500 for each budget session and $750 for each special session. In effect this was augmented over time by the legislators providing themselves a per diem of $45 for Neighbor Island members and $32.50 for legislators from Oahu. Cumulatively this was estimated to average out at about $4,385 a year, which placed Hawaii 29th among the states in 1968.

The minimum figure of $12,000 a year for a "full-time legislator" had been publicly proposed to the legislature prior to the 1968 convention by a blue-ribbon, citizens' advisory committee, which appreciated that its recommendation was in reality pointed toward influencing the public and later the convention. After considering a number of alternatives, this figure was adopted by the delegates, although not without some of the legislator members expressing grave doubts concerning its acceptability by the voters. They had good reason to believe there would not be enthusiastic public acclaim for this provision, as testified to by subsequent newspaper comments and irate letters to the editors in both Honolulu dailies. The jump in salary placed Hawaii's legislators among the top six states in the nation.

In part to meet the anticipated storm of protest, the constitutional authorization for allowances to legislators was qualified by language requiring them to be "reasonably related to expenses." To the cynical observer, this new restriction would not necessarily require any modification of the legislative allowances previously voted, but unquestionably would help make the constitutional salary increase more palatable to the voter. The following year the 1969 legislature wrestled long with the problem before scaling down the legislative per diem to correspond more closely with out-of-pocket expenses. As a safeguard against the contingency of voter rejection of the $12,000 salary, and in recognition of the difficulty any legislature faces in changing its own remuneration, the 1968 convention directed that a commission on legislative salaries, appointed by the governor, should recommend a salary plan for members of the legislature every four years. It is still left to the legislature to prescribe its own salary by the passage of a statute. Any modification in salary will not apply to the legislature which enacted it, but this does not hold for changes in allowances. This incorporation of a salary commission into the constitution is in line with a growing trend in the states. It is yet too early to know whether state legislators will willingly adopt the recc.n-mendations of such commissions; presumably they will if the normal reaction of public disapproval to legislative salary increases is countered by the fact that such increases stem from non-legislative sources.

Proposition 14 on legislative compensation, as it was included on the ballot for the voters, made no reference to the commission on legislative salaries. Instead, this was incorporated into Proposition 13 on "legislative sessions, powers, rights and procedures." The net effect of this separation was to provide Hawaii's legislators with two avenues of assistance for obtaining salary increases: one automatically at the hands of the voters should they approve Proposition 14; and the other indirectly should the commission on legislative salaries be authorized and, later, recommend that the legislature take steps to augment its annual stipend.

15. Executive Branch of Government

When the 1950 constitutional convention concluded its handiwork, it sketched for the proposed state of Hawaii an executive structure about as highly integrated as that found in any state of the Union. Observing the philosophy of the nearly half-century-old administrative reform movement and its advocacy of the short ballot, only one provision was made for the election of any administrative officers who might challenge the governor's power over the executive branch. The exception was the lieutenant governor, and he was assigned practically no constitutional duties. Plural executives for most major departments were foresworn in favor of single heads appointed by the governor. All of the executive branch was to be compressed within not more than 20 principal departments, insofar as possible each to represent a single major function.

The Committee on Executive in the 1968 convention would have carried this administrative philosophy to its logical conclusion by making cabinet posts wholly within the control of the governor (that is, both appointment and removal without the consent of the Senate, excepting only the chief legal officer of the state). With the exception of the university's board of regents and the elected board of education, collegiate heads of all other principal departments were similarly to be appointed by and subject to removal by the governor. Excluding the University of Hawaii, the Department of Education and the Hawaiian Homes Commission, the committee recommended the abolition of all plural executives. This would have affected the departments of Agriculture, and Land and Natural Resources. But what the standing committee might propose, the 1968 convention in Committee of the Whole could dispose: with the exception of empowering the governor to remove single executives without necessity of obtaining the consent of the Senate, all other modifications were deleted by the convention. Even in the exception permitted, the proviso was kept of requiring legislative consent for the removal of the chief legal officer of the state because he is also the legal adviser to the legislature.

The remaining alterations to the executive branch were minor in nature, and in some cases merely wrote existing practice into the constitution. The current salaries of the governor and lieutenant governor are now declared to be the minima; under both the 1950 constitution and as it has been changed, the legislature retains power to modify their salaries above the figure stated. The president of the University of Hawaii was exempted from the state residence requirement for department heads; the attorney general some seven years earlier had interpreted the constitution of 1950 to the same effect. In order to enable the state to draw further on talent from outside the Islands, the residence requirement for governor's appointees was reduced from three years to one. It was argued by some delegates that there should be no such requirement, but this was too radical a departure from Hawaii's traditional protectionism.

The qualifications for the office of governor, too, were relaxed, with the minimum age lowered from 35 to 30 and the required 20 years of United States citizenship eliminated. Recognizing that the selection of any age is to some extent arbitrary, the standing committee recommended the age of 30 as reasonable. The 20 years' citizenship requirement was regarded as creating an unwarranted distinction between the naturalized and native born. Citizenship remains as a requisite for voting, and, as eligibility to the office of governor depends on being a qualified voter, citizenship of an unstated minimum duration is retained by the 1968 constitution.

In other states with highly integrated executive structures such as Hawaii's, limitations on the governor succeeding himself, or on multiple terms, are protections against abuse of the executive power. Proposals to limit the number of times the governor can run for reelection were considered by the standing committee in 1968, but were all voted down on the premise that such constitutional restrictions become an expression of lack of faith in the ability of the electorate to decide intelligently whether to return to office an incumbent who has established a public record on which he may be judged. For good measure, the committee added that limited terms diminish a governor's political leadership and, as a lame-duck incumbent, he becomes ineffective as he nears the end of his allotted time. This refusal to curtail the governor's length of office only serves to highlight the extreme administrative integration possible in Hawaii's executive government.

16. The Courts

Hawaii has three levels of courts, supreme, circuit and district, the last established by statute with jurisdiction comparable to that of justices of the peace on the mainland. The attempt to raise the status of the district courts by according them constitutional recognition was not acceeded to by the Committee on the Judiciary, and the delegates in the convention did not challenge its judgment. The committee did take cognizance of the matter by urging the legislature to reorganize the courts and consider the implementation of an integrated or two-level court system. This would designate the district court as a trial court of limited jurisdiction within a division of the circuit court.

The proposal to change the method for selecting judges was supported by an organized effort to bring pressure to bear on the delegates unequalled in the 1968 convention. Interest was undoubtedly heightened by the colorful nature of the chairman of the Committee on Judiciary who, in his opposition, dramatized the issue as the staging of a play, with the implication that justice would triumph. Appointment of judges had previously characterized all of Hawaii's many forms of government. During the period of territorial status, although the justices of the supreme court and judges of the circuit courts were Washington-designated, carpetbagging was discouraged by the qualification in the Organic Act requiring a minimum three-years of residence in Hawaii. At the 1950 convention, some attention had been turned to the election of judges, considered as a radical innovation in conservative Hawaii of that day, but for the most part the delegates were content to continue the system of executive appointment subject to confirmation by the Senate. Advocates of the California or Missouri plans, which would have the gubernatorially-appointed judge running unopposed on his merits at a subsequent election, were unable to convince the 1950 convention on the merits of their position. At the 1968 convention, executive appointment of the judiciary, even though subject to the safeguard of legislative confirmation, was strenuously attacked by the advocates of the "merit" plan which places the selection of judges in the hands of a nonpartisan or bipartisan board of citizens.

The debate on the "merit" plan was protracted and heated, both outside and within the convention, initially at the hearings of the Committee on Judiciary and later on the convention floor. This issue represented the only one in which a concerted attempt was made to plan strategy long in advance of the convention, muster public interest through a Local Citizens' Administration of Justice Foundation, bring a distinguished spokesman to the state to advocate the proposed amendment before the convention, place full-page advertisements in the daily newspapers as the issue was being debated, and otherwise subject the delegates to a mass media and personal lobbying campaign associated more with the frenetic pace of the legislative chamber than the calmer deliberations of the constitutional convention hall.

Justifying the maintenance of the status quo, the majority of the Committee on Judiciary pointed to the lack of accountability to the electorate of any board of commissioners named to select judges, and referred to the existence of factional conflicts within the legal profession and the fear that one might become entrenched in the commission. The majority was not impressed by the limited adoption of the "merit" plan elsewhere in the United States. The proponents of the plan cited in its favor that it had received the sanction of the American Bar Association and the American Judicature Society, and attempted to prove that its acceptance was growing on the mainland. They urged in support of their position that the use of the commission would permit selection of judges free of the influence of partisan politics, with both lawyer and layman being used in the selection process. Detrimental to their cause, however, was the lack of any allegation that the current method for naming judges had been abused or had brought incompetents to the bench. From the standpoint of tactics, the very fact that the members of the Hawaii bar were almost evenly split over the desirability of the commission plan also weakened the advocates' case.

The obvious collection of funds for financing the advertising campaign, the appearance of favorable editorials in both Honolulu dailies within one day of each other, and the concerted efforts at bringing organized pressure to bear on the delegates all backfired. Given the limited citizen interest, the division of views among the legal profession, and the apparent threat to political rewards and punishments should the present system be modified, uncommitted delegates were more repelled than attracted to the cause.

Twelve members supported the chairman of the Committee on Judiciary in recommending retention of the status quo. Ten members dissented, and nine of them later signed a minority report advocating the adoption of a commission for selecting judges. The Committee of the Whole rejected a "diluted" amendment which would have established a commission to screen candidates and submit a list of qualified persons to the governor, who would then nominate for confirmation by the Senate. When the last vote was taken and the issue resolved, the question remained of how much the unusual structuring of the Committee on Judiciary's membership had contributed to the defeat of the "merit" plan.

A much less volatile issue was the changing of judges' terms of service. The length of term of the judges of the circuit courts and justices of the supreme court being fixed by the constitution, this could not be left to the ministrations of the legislature. Since the delegates desired to attract the best candidates, in order to provide greater incentives for practicing attorneys to leave lucrative law practices, to insulate judges for longer periods of time from the pressures of reappointment, and to ensure greater accrual of retirement pension benefits, they lengthened to 10 years the terms of circuit court judges (from six years) and supreme court justices (from seven years). The delegates also wished to guard against the perpetuation of "bad" judges. Recognizing that the legislature had yet failed to enact implementing legislation under the 1950 constitution establishing cause for the removal from office of members of the bench, the convention proposed that removal for cause, as well as retirement for incapacity, should be inquired into by a commission appointed by the governor. On its recommendation, the governor is directed to remove or retire the judicial officer.

Following the same pattern as applied in the case of executive officers, the convention also wrote into the constitution as minimum salaries the amounts being paid to the judiciary; although the legislature may subsequently change judges' remuneration, it may not reduce below the constitutional minimum. Finally, to provide an additional roster of candidates to sit temporarily on the supreme court, the chief justice is empowered to call on retired justices. Through this device the temporary assignment of circuit judges to the appellate body becomes unnecessary, avoiding further augmentation of the backlog of cases in the circuit courts as well as placing the judge in the sometimes embarrassing situation of overruling the decisions of his peers.

17. Debt Ceiling

Since annexation, public indebtedness in Hawaii has about tripled every 20 years, and in the near decade after statehood the rate of increase has been even faster. Under the 1950 constitution the ceiling set for state debt was tied to the net assessed valuation of real property. As property tax revenues go to the counties, and are expended by them, the 1968 convention's Committee on Taxation and Finance termed a state debt ceiling so phrased as "an affront to reason." Instead, because non-reimbursable state general obligation bonds are repaid out of general funds, it was believed logical to tie the constitutional debt ceiling to some measure of the money available to cover debt service charges. After considerable debate the committee agreed on a multiple of three and one-half times the state's general fund revenues averaged over a three-year period. This represented the equivalent of immediately raising the state debt ceiling by about 66⅔ percent, which prompted the committee to add that this did not set the measure, nor constitute a substitute for good debt policy and effective debt management, but only to provide a margin for flexibility and unforeseen contingencies.

For the counties, 15 percent of the total assessed values for real property taxes is fixed as the limit for their funded debt. This is a 50 percent increase over the 1950 constitutional limit and immediately benefits the Neighbor Island counties by providing them a larger dollar margin judged necessary because of their low level of property values. The restriction in the 1950 constitution, raising a 2 percent limit on the amount of new debt issued in any one year was also removed.

Other bond changes ran to the classification of revenue bonds, as distinct from general obligation bonds, and the handling of obligations for the funding of undertakings from which revenues will ultimately be realized. The net effect of all these changes was to liberalize the fiscal restraints written into the 1950 constitution, and at the same time rewrite the provisions applicable to public debt so as to tie them to more realistic measures. It is doubtful that the average citizen could understand either the technical language in which the constitutional changes were phrased or even the "non-legal language" used to explain the modifications.

18. State Budgets and Appropriations

The delegates to the constitutional convention of 1950 innovatively proposed annual state budgeting, and directed the separation of operating expenses from capital expenditures. Eighteen years later the second convention recommended that Hawaii return to a biennial budget to improve planning, permit the legislature to engage in more intensive analyses in the non-budget years, and "to alleviate the administrative burden of almost perpetual involvement in the existing annual budgeting process." Even the requirement that the capital budget be separated from the operating budget was deleted, permitting greater flexibility. Now left to the legislature is full discretion for prescribing the budget form and process, with many of the delegates assuming this will facilitate institution of a planning-programing-budgeting system. Realistically, the delegates knew that, with biennial budgeting restored, requests for supplemental appropriations would be made in the intervening year. Should such supplemental appropriation bills be introduced, they are to be assigned the same priority for passage as the general appropriations bills implementing the executive budget. Hawaii thus joined Georgia, the only other state with annual legislative sessions and a biennial budget.

This amendment represents a full turnabout in constitutional logic: the 1950 convention's proposal of the annual session, restricted in the even-numbered year so that attention was focused on the budget, was originally justified as necessary to permit annual budgeting. Now, as a result of the 1968 amendments, full legislative sessions are to be the order each year, while biennial budgeting has been reinstituted. No one anticipates that the new budgetary directions will preclude the legislature from adopting during the interim budgetary period extensive revisions to both operating and capital improvements appropriations. This will in effect retain a degree of annual legislative oversight of the budget even though the executive now returns to biennial formulation and execution.

19. Local Government; Charters

The 1950 constitution authorized political subdivisions to adopt charters under procedures to be prescribed by the legislature. This did not constitute a grant of "home rule," and such charters have been held subject to continuing legislative controls. By way of "adding insult to injury" for those championing local government, this constitutional provision also did not preclude the legislature from making special provision governing the adoption of each charter.

The announced drive by county officials to have the constitution lodge greater discretionary powers in the local governments had more staged performance than substantive support. Compared with the mainland, local government in Hawaii has always rendered few functions, while the most costly activities—education, health, transportation and welfare—are almost entirely state responsibilities. The county officials knew this long-run trend of government ran against their effort to readjust the balance. Besides, they labored under two immediate disadvantages:

(a) there was no true united front among the counties, for the Neighbor Islands do not have the financial capacity to sustain the cost of any major reassignment of functions to the localities;

(b) their arguments had to be pitched to a standing committee of the convention which was chaired by a state senator and on which nine other incumbent state legislators sat. In the absence of any strong dissatisfaction from the citizenry, or advantages to be gained by organized interests from decentralization, the position of the "Hawaii State Association of Counties" was foredoomed.

Currently, Hawaii's constitution specifies that each political subdivision shall have those powers which are conferred under general laws. It was the counties' position that the constitution ought to be reoriented to place residual powers in the local government, that is, the counties should enjoy all powers not denied them by charter, statute or constitution. When pushed to elaborate on what they would do with residual powers, spokesmen for the counties could agree on little more than that the counties might experiment with new taxes. Under the constitution the taxing power, also, is reserved to the state, except as delegated by the legislature to the political subdivisions. The convention delegates were in no mood to augment local fiscal powers, and were of the same persuasion with regard to residual powers once the impact of that change was admitted.

Simply put, additional taxing powers were not to be granted unless major functional powers were assigned to the local governmental units. But, as noted, the Neighbor Island counties lack an economic base to support such functions. The state is not about to allow the city and county of Honolulu to levy local taxes without regard to their statewide impact, nor to establish a functional structure which breaks the near-century-long pattern of uniformity by assigning responsibility for some functions to the state outside of Honolulu, and to the city and county on Oahu. Very early in the hearings, lack of unanimity among the various counties in pushing for augmented powers was revealed, and by the end the counties' position had been reduced to almost a rout. Representatives of local government, bulwarked by the stands taken by private citizen groups, were lucky to win incorporation of the limited improvements designed to protect against further arbitrary action by the legislature.

In the future, general laws must oversee the adoption of local self-government charters. The procedures to be established may not call for the submission of the charter to either the state or existing local legislative bodies. This will leave the electorate of the subdivision as the sole ratifying agency although, of course, not precluding legislative-proposed amendments to existing charters.

With a narrowly defined area, the delegates also proposed to afford county charters higher status than state statutes. Using as a model the recommendations of the American Municipal Association (now National League of Cities), the constitutional amendment places beyond state control those charter provisions which govern the executive, legislative, and administrative structure and organization of the political subdivision. Although the form of local government can no longer become a matter of state concern, the legislature retains authority to enact general laws allocating and reallocating powers and functions. Coupled with the fact that the total taxing power is still lodged in the state and available to local units only by legislative action, this 1968 constitutional change will accomplish little more than precluding the most venal form of political interference by state legislators in local governmental affairs. Even this restraint is somewhat questionable as the constitution now defines "general laws" in such manner that they need not be applicable to all of the counties, but may relate to only one.

Honolulu's charter was adopted before the effective date of the 1950 constitutional provisions; those for the three Neighbor Island counties were drawn up under enabling statutes governed by the state constitution. To tidy this all up the 1968 convention declares that the language of the amended constitution is to apply to all county charters, but, as a safeguard, delayed the effective date of the local government amendments for three years. This served to reserve to the state legislature both power to review the new charters just completed in the Neighbor Islands and opportunity for it to pass on reapportionment of the Honolulu city and county council, a political issue at the time of the convention. Just as the delegates saw little reason to revise the centralization of government which has so long characterized public administration in the Islands, so, too, there seemed little need drastically or immediately to curtail the state legislature's long political involvement in local governmental affairs.

20. Collective Bargaining for Public Employees

In 1950 the delegates wrote into Hawaii's constitution the right of persons in private employment to organize for the purpose of collective bargaining. Such a right for public employees was yet too novel, but Hawaii's first state constitution did declare that those persons could organize and make their grievances and proposals known. In 1968 the delegates returned to the same problem and further narrowed the difference between the rights of public and private employees.

The proposal as given to the voters merely states that "persons in public employment shall have the right to organize for the purpose of collective bargaining as prescribed by law." In the words of the convention's Committee on Style, "The meaning of this sentence is not crystal clear in itself." To the standing committee which sponsored the amendment, "collective bargaining" for public employees is not identical with that of private employees, but restricted to those areas and exercisable in such manner as has been determined by the legislature. This left for legislative determination the question of whether public employees may engage in strikes. The attorney general assured the delegates that pertinent statutes, including those prohibiting strikes by public employees, would remain effective until changes were enacted by the legislature. After protracted debate in the Committee of the Whole, the majority of the delegates indicated their willingness to transfer the whole subject to the legislature for resolution. Consonant with this spirit, a proposal to add a "right-to-work" amendment to the constitution was defeated, the same standing committee indicating that this objective could be accomplished by legislative enactment should it be considered desirable to take such action.

21. Codes of Ethics; Disloyalty Disqualification

The "do-gooder" concerned with government sometimes occupies the dubious position of serving as the citizen's conscience, but in such a politically unsophisticated manner as to make his efficacy suspect. The constitutional direction that the state legislature and each political subdivision adopt a code of ethics for appointed and elected officers and employees represents the handiwork of the "do-gooder." It should be added, however, that in this case results were achieved not despite political ineptitude but because of well-laid plans which secured broad community backing for the proposal.

A citizens' committee, supported by the League of Women Voters and some other church groups, has for a number of years campaigned for the adoption of ethics codes in both state and local government. A state statute and local charter provisions can be traced to its efforts. Their coverage does not extend as broadly as that which the constitutional provision now contemplates, but it would appear to ensure their continuance; eventually they will be replaced by new codes of ethics for all public employees and officers.

When Hawaii's first constitution was drafted, the spirit of McCarthyism was still strong and the work of the convention was conducted against the backdrop of charges of rampant communism. One of the direct results was the incorporation into the 1950 constitution of a section barring from public office or employment any person advocating the overthrow of the government by force and violence, or who aids or belongs to an organization with such purpose. In the intervening years, judicial opinion challenged the constitutionality of such broad language, and the delegates in 1968 were assured of its invalidity by the attorney general. The convention's standing committee concluded that a disqualification for disloyalty ought still to be contained in the constitution and proposed substitute language limiting it to persons knowingly and intentionally acting, attempting or conspiring to overthrow the government by force or violence. Advised that the proposal met the test of constitutionality, the substitute section was submitted to the convention and accepted after a further attempt to reduce its scope to delete the ban on employment. The impression gained was that the entire subject would have been omitted from the constitution and left for legislative action if the delegates had not feared this course of action might raise a volatile issue which would constitute an unnecessary obstacle to the favorable reception of the convention's amendments by the voters.

22. Revision and Amendments to the Constitution

When the convention of 1950 was concluding its work, it wrote into the constitution that future conventions should have the same number of delegates elected from the same areas, and be convened in the same manner, unless the legislature were to provide otherwise. The legislature did so in 1968. This convention anticipated its successors, also specifying that they were to be in its image unless the legislature decided otherwise. The delegates went one step farther than their predecessors, however, by indicating that future constitutional conventions should have the same powers and privileges as those enjoyed in 1968, in the absence of legislation to the contrary.

As to the question of ratification of the convention's handiwork, the original state constitution requires not only an affirmative majority of all of the votes tallied, but also that such majority must constitute at least 35 percent of the total vote cast if a general election, or 35 percent of the total number of registered voters if at a special election. Since turnout at special elections tends to be light, the possibility is poor for obtaining the high percentage needed to ratify a constitutional amendment. The 1968 convention reduced to 30 the percentage of registered voters at a special election, a conservative amendment which raised no objection when brought to the floor of the convention.

Originally the constitution had attempted to foreclose amendments altering senatorial representation unless an extraordinary majority was obtained. Clearly unconstitutional, in that it permitted a minority of the population to prevent the reapportionment of the Senate, the 1968 delegates removed this provision.

The 1968 convention knew that its reapportionment recommendations would be measured against those previously submitted by the legislature and that the electorate would be called on to choose between them. To avoid confusion, and not so incidentally to give priority to their handiwork, the delegates inserted language into the revised constitution declaring that, irrespective of the vote cast, proposals from a constitutional convention, if carried, controlled over conflicting amendments or revisions proposed by the legislature. In the case of conflicting provisions proposed by the same body, and submitted to the voters at the same election, the amendment or revision receiving the highest number of affirmative votes is to prevail. At the vote on the constitution in the 1968 elections the convention's proposed reapportionment plan received a higher tally than did the legislative proposal, even though the latter also obtained the requisite majority. As a consequence, under the normal rules of construction, even in the absence of the novel constitutional provision giving priority to the convention, the convention's plan would have been controlling. Whether or not there ever will be occasion again to apply this unusual language remains questionable.

23. *Technical and Transitional Amendments*

Lumped together as a single "highlight" was a motley collection of deletions and rewordings of obsolete or unconstitutional sections, style changes, and incidental amendments to facilitate modifications in the other "highlights." In all, Hawaii's voters repealed 12 sections of the constitution on the premise that this tidied up the new document. Although obviously not understanding the intricacies of what was being accomplished, the voters accepted these changes as technical and non-substantive.

Other changes in the content of the constitution would have been incorporated if several sizable groupings of delegates could have had their way. A move to repeal the elected board of education never received committee approval, while the standing committee's recommendation to write advisory school committees into the constitution was defeated in Committee of the Whole. Proposals for constitutional specification of the state seal, song (Hawaii Ponoi), flower (Hibiscus) and bird (Nene) were all placed on file. At the 1950 convention a motion to include the state seal in the constitution was defeated in an effort to avoid cluttering it with detail. On similar grounds, and to avoid the possibility that other heraldic symbols might be proposed, such as the state motto, nickname, tree or color, the 1968 Committee on Revision, Amendment and Other Provisions would have none of it, nor would the convention.

The sum total of the amendments adopted, or even seriously studied, supports only one conclusion: the general attitude of the 1968 convention tended toward minimal change. The delegates were not disposed toward basic reconsideration of the constitution, and in the main were satisfied with minor, corrective adjustments. In the introduction to proposed "Constitutional Provisions on Taxation and Finance," prepared for the 1950 convention, the Tax Study Committee of the Honolulu Chamber of Commerce declared: "Hawaii's government needs evolutionary improvement, not revolutionary change." And, as to modifications, "they must be tempered by a close examination of the local situation." This well epitomized the underlying philosophy of both the 1950 constitutional convention and that which met in 1968.

9.

Selling the Constitution

There are two basic ways to submit the work of a constitutional convention to popular referendum. It may be presented to the electorate as a single proposition to be accepted or rejected as a whole. This is the method finally adopted in 1950, when voters were faced with the question: "Shall the proposed Constitution of the State of Hawaii be adopted? Yes ☐ No ☐." The alternative is to submit the constitutional proposals piecemeal, with each individual article or amendment adopted on its own merits. All other forms of referenda are only variants or combinations of the two. In 1968, Hawaii employed a novel approach premised on the amendment-by-amendment method, but also incorporating features allied to a single endorsement of the entire constitution. Both times the method of submission was determined by the convention, but in 1950 this need not have occurred.

The legislation which set up the statehood convention mandated that the draft constitution be reviewed by the territorial legislature before going to the voters. The legislators could then submit alternative and additional provisions. The delegate to Congress suggested that this feature be bypassed, and the convention delegates did not take kindly to this reserved power of review. By resolution the convention noted that the draft it had prepared was an integrated document, and expressed the hope that if the legislature were to suggest alternative proposals, they would be presented to the people as a whole. In this way the electorate could choose between two complete drafts and not a myriad of details.

118

1950: Timetable for Submission

With the constitution signed, the immediate problem was whether to call a special legislative session on petition so that the document could be voted on at the forthcoming November general election, or wait until the following year when the next regular session would meet. Rumor had it that the governor opposed convening a special session; some legislators claimed that placing the constitution on the ballot in November would be unfair to the voter, mixing party politics, election of candidates and constitutional ratification. More potent was the argument that signing a petition for the special session would demonstrate the strength of the statehood cause, as this would hurry the popular vote and consequent confrontation of Washington with the approved document. Those who opposed the special session because of additional cost were answered by the extra cost of a special election which would be required for the referendum in 1951 should the proposed constitution be held over for consideration at the next regular session.

A legislative clerk flew around the territory obtaining legislators' signatures. Eventually, eight out of 15 senators and 25 of the then 29 representatives endorsed the petition. When the governor called the special session, addressing the members in joint session, he referred to the constitution as "on the whole . . . an excellent document," but proposed that the legislators review its contents: the enlarged state legislature would be unwieldy in size, cumbersome and expensive; the provision for annual meeting of the legislature ought to be carefully reconsidered; and Neighbor Islands' domination of the Senate, in view of their small population, should be corrected. The legislators thus faced the dilemma of being charged with rubber stamping the constitutional convention if they did nothing, and being accused of sabotaging statehood if they proposed alternatives. In addition they understood full well that opening up the compromises reached in convention on the state legislature might preclude coming to any agreement.

The Committee on Submission and Information delegated a subcommittee to work with the legislature on the constitution, and urge its adoption. The ILWU submitted a 14-point objection to the draft constitution, protesting the haste with which legislative approval was proceeding, but it represented a minority voice. Some of the legislator-delegates who had opposed provisions in the convention now fought for the constitution as an entirety and against incorporating any legislative alternatives. Their strongest argument was avoidance of voter confusion, to permit an overwhelming "yes" vote. Unanimously the House found the constitution ac-

ceptable and approved its submission without any additions or alternatives; the Senate followed suit with only two dissenting "nays." Instead of
a series of provisions the voters would receive a ballot with a single
question, adoption of the constitution.

The work of the 1950 Committee on Submission and Information was
considerably eased by this legislative decision. With the convention concluded, the committee's size was increased from 15 to 21 members. A
series of releases on the articles of the proposed constitution was written
by the delegates and published in the newspapers. The committee arranged for delegates to appear before clubs and other interested groups,
and radio presentations also furthered the pre-election educational campaign.

1950: The Campaign

The committee had to rely mainly on volunteer services, for only $6,500
remained available for expenditure. At the special session another $5,000
was appropriated to pay the cost of printing the whole constitution in
Honolulu's two daily newspapers. (The special session also appropriated
$75,000 for the constitutional convention to reconvene in the event that
the voters rejected the constitution.) During the last three weeks before
the election the drive to "sell" the constitution was quickened. The committee distributed a pamphlet summarizing the constitution's highlights
and answering the ILWU's objections. Sample ratification ballots were
broadcast widely. "Constitution Week" was observed in the schools just
prior to the general election, and studies of the proposed document were
encouraged. Copies of the document were widely distributed, including
to the schools for students to take home to their parents.

Only the ILWU actively and openly opposed the ratification of the
constitution: Apportionment of the legislature should be based not on
"registered voters" but on population; the legislature was too unwieldy,
and granting it power to disqualify its own members and punish non-
members was unwise; the governor should have the right to remove his
own appointees without need of Senate consent; judges and more
executive officers should be elected; bond issues and other large expenditures should be submitted to popular vote, and provision included
for initiative, referendum and recall; the "speak, read and write English
or Hawaiian" qualification for voters ought to have been stricken; free
public education should have been mandated, as well as effective administration of the Hawaiian Homes Commission. In all this was a mas-

sive indictment and the union carried its attack through personal contact, printed publications and radio statements.

But the ILWU's was a lonely voice. Otherwise, all organized effort flowed in the opposite direction, with such organizations as the Hawaii Education Association and the various Island chambers of commerce endorsing the constitution and urging their members to vote "yes." University of Hawaii students at a mock election voted 10 to 1 in favor of adopting the constitution. Editorials in both Honolulu daily newspapers recommended ratification, and the voters were assured that this was an important step toward achieving statehood. A negative vote could be anticipated from some Hawaiian groups and others not pleased with that prospect, but they failed to make common cause in opposing the constitution.

1950: The Vote

On November 7, 1950, 118,767 citizens went to the polls, and 109,897 voted the separate ballot which carried the state constitutional question. A strong majority (82,788) opted for adoption, three times as many as the 27,109 who voted against the constitution. In 155 of the territory's 166 election precincts, the constitution received a favorable vote. The negative campaign of the ILWU—"vote no if you have not read the Draft Constitution"—and the covert resistance to statehood found in pockets of unorganized opposition explain the bulk of the negative vote.

Now was to come nearly a decade of marking time, waiting for the U. S. Congress to acknowledge the proposed constitution concurrent with admitting Hawaii as a state. Before this, the enlarged legislature and the districting provisions of the new constitution were grafted onto the Organic Act to preclude judicial inquiry into the territorial legislature's malapportionment. Later, after Hawaii became a state, these very directions for apportioning the legislature were to be challenged, and action thereon by a federal court led to setting up the constitutional convention of 1968.

1968: Submission—Similarities and Differences

Paradoxically, the delegates to the 1968 convention faced a problem at the same time more complex and simpler than did the 1950 convention. The state constitution had now been in force for nearly a decade and had proven its fundamental soundness. The ILWU had abandoned its position calling for massive amendments, and there would be no com-

parable organized opposition. (Of the ILWU's original objections, two
were accommodated by the 1968 amendments: gubernatorial removal
of appointees and elimination of the literacy requirement to vote.) On
the other hand, there was no longer any movement similar to the statehood drive to carry the convention's handiwork along as an adjunct to
the main current. There would be little disagreement by the voters with
the majority of changes the 1968 convention proposed, but, then again,
these amendments were not attention-getting by nature. Each might,
indeed, receive a majority of votes cast, and still run afoul of the constitution's requirement of a minimum tied to the total vote cast. As for
the controversial amendments, such as lowering the voting age to 18 and
increasing legislators' salaries to $12,000, including them with all other
changes in a single package might bring defeat to the entire revision.

The 1968 convention enjoyed full discretion in deciding how and when
to present its proposals to the voters. Before the delegates assembled the
attorney general had ruled in response to an inquiry that the convention
had carte blanche power. As the work of the convention proceeded, however, it became evident that it would be impossible to submit each
amendment separately; by the time the convention had completed its review of the constitution's 16 articles, over one-third of the sections
had been amended, added to or renumbered. Approximately 34 amendments would have to be listed if each divisible item were submitted individually. Some grouping would be requisite should the entire revision
not be presented as a unit. But the recent debacles in Maryland, New
York and Rhode Island disclosed the risk to be run if all of the convention's effort could be defeated by subjecting it to a simple "yes" or "no"
vote.

The 1968 Committee on Submission and Information wrestled long
with the problem. The program it would mount for educating the Islanders on the proposed constitutional revision would depend on the format
for framing the ballot question. The form which the ballot should take
turned on voters' attitudes toward the convention, the size of the opposition to specific provisions, and the extent to which apathy might
contribute to the failure to receive the requisite 35 percent of the total
vote cast (if submitted at a general election) or of the registered voters
(if a special election were used as the vehicle). All this in part would be
influenced by the post-convention educational campaign, and so the
committee was back at its starting point.

The committee had as its objectives securing approval of a maximum
number of items while enabling the voter to feel he had a chance to express his free choice, agreeing on an understandable ballot, and setting

up the voting procedure in such manner as not to be time consuming. Legal counsel recommended against any arbitrary grouping on the ballot; the voter had to be permitted a reasonable opportunity to pick and choose, should more than a single "yes-no" vote be called for. The lieutenant governor pointed out the difficulty of employing lengthy proposals with either mechanical voting machines or the electronic voting system. Originally it was believed that only a maximum of eight proposals could be included on one side of the punch-card ballot of the electronic voting system, but later this was expanded, and eventually it accommodated 17 proposals on a single side, plus instructions on voting.

Contributing to the Committee on Submission and Information's difficulties was its large and atypical composition, with chairmen of all other convention committees included ex officio. After the members present at one meeting had tentatively agreed to the ballot form, the same ground would be covered again at the next meeting, when members not previously present would contest the conclusions. Meanwhile, pressure mounted in the convention to reach a decision. The committee chairman proposed a six-item ballot (vote for 18-year-olds, removal of the literacy requirement, legislative salaries, collective bargaining for public employees, reapportionment and all other amendments). President Porteus spoke for six or seven groupings and, through a strong educational program, for gaining the support of legislative and business organizations. Others advocated submission of the constitutional revision as a single unit. Repeatedly, the designation in committee of any particular item for separate presentation drew the objection of constituting an arbitrary exclusion of another, equally deserving of itemization on the ballot. Finally, consensus was reached on a three-part ballot, with the voter able to express approval for or reject the entire revision, and a third portion allowing the voter to negate any of the grouped amendments, but otherwise have his ballot counted as being in favor of all proposals for which he failed to express a "no" vote. The "yes, no, and yes—but" ballot promised to be particularly well-phrased for satisfying the 35 percent qualification. The average voter, desiring to oppose one or more amendments, normally would not bother to vote on all of the remainder in view of their lacking political saliency; these proposals without "no" votes would be included in the "yes" count. A subcommittee grouped all of the constitutional changes into 23 proposals and, after some minor rearrangements, all these passed the scrutiny of the parent committee and the attorney general, as did the ballot form. Later the lieutenant governor arranged for the punch-card ballot to carry only the 23 proposal titles, while a separate sheet described the issues in greater detail. A sample ballot follows.

SAMPLE BALLOT

Please note your choice and take it with you to the polls.

PART A – If you vote in Part A you will be voting Yes on all of the questions.

PART B – If you choose Part B you will be voting No on all of the questions.

PART C – If you vote in Part C you will have a listing of twenty-three questions. Your vote will be counted as a Yes vote, except where you choose to mark a No vote.

In order to save you some time at your polling place, we encourage you to study the Proposed Amendments to the Hawaii State Constitution (in back) ahead of time. When you have made your decisions, we recommend that you mark your choice or choices on this sample ballot and take it with you to your polling place. By following your pre-marked sample ballot as you vote, you will complete your voting sooner, thus preventing long waiting lines.

DISTRIBUTED BY
OFFICE OF THE LIEUTENANT GOVERNOR
STATE OF HAWAII

OFFICIAL BALLOT

Amendments to the State Constitution proposed by the 1968 Constitutional Convention

November 5, 1968 — State of Hawaii

Please read instructions and information in the booklet which is part of this ballot. The full text of the amendments covered by the ballot questions is available for inspection in your voting unit.

DO NOT REMOVE THIS STUB

Vote only in Part A or Part B or Part C
DO NOT VOTE IN MORE THAN ONE PART

PART A
I vote **YES** on each of the questions on the amendments to the Hawaii State Constitution proposed by the 1968 Constitutional Convention as listed under Part C and numbered 1—23, inclusive.

Yes on Each ⊕

PART B
I vote **NO** on each of the questions on the amendments to the Hawaii State Constitution proposed by the 1968 Constitutional Convention as listed under Part C and numbered 1—23, inclusive.

No on Each ⊕

PART C
I vote **YES** on each of the questions on the amendments to the Hawaii State Constitution proposed by the 1968 Constitutional Convention as listed below and numbered 1—23, inclusive, **EXCEPT** that I vote **NO** on one or more of the questions as follows:

1.	Apportionment and Districting of Legislature	No ⊕
2.	Provisions for Future Reapportionment	No ⊕
3.	Minimum Representation for Basic Island Units	No ⊕
4.	Guarantees Against Unreasonable Invasions of Privacy	No ⊕
5.	Allow Courts to Dispense with Bail Under Certain Conditions	No ⊕
6.	Counsel for Indigents	No ⊕

CONTINUE ON OTHER SIDE (OVER)

-5-68 **VOTE BOTH SIDES** (OVER)

BEGIN ON OTHER SIDE OF THIS CARD

Please read instructions and information in the booklet which is part of this ballot. The full text of the amendments covered by the ballot questions is available for inspection in your voting unit.

DO NOT REMOVE THIS STUB

CONTINUED FROM OTHER SIDE

7.	Payment for Certain Damages to Private Property	No ⊕
8.	Eighteen Year Old Vote	No ⊕
9.	Voting Rights of Felons	No ⊕
10.	Eliminating the Literacy Requirement to Vote	No ⊕
11.	Authorization for Presidential Preference Primary	No ⊕
12.	Minimum Age of Legislators	No ⊕
13.	Legislative Sessions, Powers, Rights and Procedures	No ⊕
14.	Legislative Compensation	No ⊕
15.	Eligibility of Governor; Compensation of Governor and Lt. Governor; Removal of Single Executives and Certain Other Officers; Residence Requirement for Appointed Officials	No ⊕
16.	Judicial Administration, Term of Office and Compensation	No ⊕
17.	State and County Debt Limits	No ⊕
18.	Two Year Budgeting and Appropriations	No ⊕
19.	Local Government; Charter; Effective Date	No ⊕
20.	Collective Bargaining for Public Employees	No ⊕
21.	Code of Ethics and Disqualification for Disloyalty	No ⊕
22.	Revisions and Amendments to the Constitution	No ⊕
23.	Technical, Transitional, Style and Other Changes	No ⊕

VOTE BOTH SIDES

KNOW THE ISSUES...THEN VOTE ON THE AMENDMENTS TO HAWAII'S CONSTITUTION

THESE ARE THE HIGHLIGHTS OF THE PROPOSED AMENDMENTS TO THE HAWAII STATE CONSTITUTION

THE PROPOSED CHANGES	WHY A CHANGE WAS RECOMMENDED
1. APPORTIONMENT AND DISTRICTING OF LEGISLATURE. Sets up new House and Senate districts (Con-Con plan) to take effect in the 1970 election. Seats in the Legislature have been reallocated so that each legislator is elected by approximately the same number of registered voters. (If the Con-Con plan and the Legislature's plan for reapportionment are both approved the Con-Con plan will take effect.)	To reapportion the State Legislature to comply with the "one man, one vote" decisions of the U.S. Supreme Court. The goal of these Supreme Court decisions is to reapportion districts in such a way that each legislator will represent by approximately the same number of voters. Hawaii has the option of straightening out its own apportionment or having a court do it for them.
2. PROVISIONS FOR FUTURE REAPPORTIONMENT. Beginning in 1973, a nine-man commission would be appointed every 8 years and given the job of revising and updating the State's legislative apportionment.	To insure an automatic means of bringing apportionment in line with Hawaii's changing population. Already in use in several states, the commission system will insure that an independent panel is selected to review population trends at 8-year intervals so Hawaii's Legislature will continue to reflect its population.
3. MINIMUM REPRESENTATION FOR BASIC ISLAND UNITS. No county will ever be allotted less than 2 senators and 3 representatives. When a county's representation falls below the minimum, additional seats will be allocated to bring it up to that minimum. In such a case, each senator or representative would have only a fractional vote (in 1970, Kauai would have 2 senators, each with one-half vote).	To insure that each section of the State has a delegation to the Legislature sufficient to present its views in the many committees. The Neighbor Island counties, whose populations have not grown as fast as Oahu's, are thus assured of having a workable minimum number of legislators at the State Capitol.
4. GUARANTEES AGAINST UNREASONABLE INVASIONS OF PRIVACY. This new addition to the Bill of Rights would guarantee additional protection for citizens against "unreasonable invasions of privacy". For instance, no wiretapping or "bugging" could be done without a court order.	Although court decisions and statutes already enforce certain parts of this "right of privacy", the increasing use of electronic devices and the enlargement of government's role in modern life require that there be constitutional protection of each citizen's privacy.
5. ALLOW COURTS TO DISPENSE WITH BAIL UNDER CERTAIN CONDITIONS. This new addition to the Bill of Rights would allow a judge to do away with bail in cases where he is satisfied the defendant or witness will appear in court when ordered to do so. Offenses involving possible life imprisonment, however, are excluded from this provision.	Because the only reason for bail is to guarantee that a defendant or witness appears at the trial. In reality, however, it often has worked to the disadvantage of the poor. If a judge is reasonably sure that a defendant or witness will appear, there is no reason to require bail. This system is already used to some extent in Hawaii courts.
6. COUNSEL FOR INDIGENTS.	To insure that no defendant is denied the help of a lawyer simply because of lack of funds. The U.S...

THE PROPOSED CHANGES	WHY A CHANGE WAS RECOMMENDED
14. LEGISLATIVE COMPENSATION. Adjust legislators' pay to $12,000 per year until changed after recommendation of a new salary commission.	Salaries have not been adjusted since 1950. The present low salary ($4,000 for two years) makes it prohibitive for many persons to seek public office. A salary increase will encourage additional qualified people to seek legislative office.
15. GOVERNOR; LT. GOVERNOR; REMOVAL OF CABINET EXECUTIVES. *Lowers age minimum for the Governor to 30 years (from 35). *Sets minimum salaries for Governor and Lt. Governor at the present pay levels. *Allows Governor to remove cabinet members (except Attorney General) without Senate approval.	*Lower age minimum brings Hawaii in line with 44 other states and broadens the choice of voters. *A salary minimum protects the Governor from legislative action to lower his pay unreasonably. *Governor should have power to decide who will remain in his official "family" without gaining Senate approval.
16. JUDICIAL ADMINISTRATION, TERM OF OFFICE, COMPENSATION. *Lengthens judges' terms of office to 10 years (from 6 and 7 years). *Allows the Chief Justice to ask retired justices to sit on Supreme Court as needed to fill short-term vacancies. *Sets up an independent commission for removal of judges.	*Longer terms will increase courts' independence and induce highly-qualified lawyers to accept judgeships. Permits judges and justices to qualify for retirement benefits after serving one full term. *Use of retired justices will reduce the need to have already-overburdened Circuit Court judges sit on the Supreme Court. *A special commission strengthens the provisions for removing judges who may be incapacitated or otherwise unfit to hold judicial office.
17. STATE AND COUNTY DEBT LIMITS. Ties the State debt ceiling to State income (general fund revenues) rather than to real property values. This will increase the limit on both State and county borrowing.	Relating the State borrowing limit to its income is a more realistic measure of the State's ability to pay off debt. An increased debt limit insures that government will be able to provide the facilities needed by Hawaii's growing population.
18. TWO YEAR BUDGETING AND APPROPRIATIONS. Beginning in 1971, the State's annual budgeting system would be replaced by a biennial (two-year) budget, with appropriations being reviewed each year by the Governor and Legislature.	Eliminates the need for a repetitive annual budgeting procedure and permits more intensive review of those areas of expenditure which need analysis. Promotes for integration with planning, programming and budgeting systems.

into Hawaii's Constitution and further extend the safeguard to defendants in most minor cases (misdemeanors).

over their charters and internal organization within the limits prescribed by general law. The Legislature would not be able to control or veto county actions relating to their internal structures.

to handle their internal matters without control and review by the State Legislature. This change allows each county government to organize itself to meet its unique needs.

7. PAYMENT FOR CERTAIN DAMAGES TO PRIVATE PROPERTY.

This addition to the Bill of Rights would require the government to pay for damage it causes to private property in connection with a "public" project—such as a highway. At the present time the government must pay only if it physically takes land in eminent domain cases.

Paying only for land "taken," while ignoring other damages or loss of value to landowners, appeared to be an artificial and unjust distinction.

8. EIGHTEEN YEAR OLD VOTE.

This amendment would lower Hawaii's minimum voting age from 20 to 18 years.

Young people today generally are better educated than ever before and have a substantial knowledge of politics and candidates. Many assume the duties of adulthood by the age of 18 and they should be allowed a voice in government by being given the privilege of voting.

9. VOTING RIGHT OF FELONS.

This would restore the right to vote to felons at the time of their final discharge, which is the completion of their prison term, plus any parole or probation (even earlier if the Legislature would so provide). Now, a felon is forever barred from voting unless he receives a pardon from the Governor.

This amendment recognizes the fact that our prison system is designed to rehabilitate felons. After their release, they ought to re-enter society and feel that they are playing a full role in it. Excluding them from voting emphasizes their second class status and hinders rehabilitation.

10. ELIMINATING THE LITERACY REQUIREMENT TO VOTE.

The present Constitution requires that a citizen be able to "speak, read and write English or Hawaiian" in order to vote. The amendment would delete this requirement completely.

Radio and television make it possible for an illiterate person to learn about issues and candidates. Furthermore, Hawaii has many citizens non-literate in English or Hawaiian, but literate in Japanese or a Filipino dialect, for instance, who have their own language newspapers, television and radio programs to acquaint them with politics.

11. AUTHORIZATION FOR PRESIDENTIAL PREFERENCE PRIMARY.

This would allow but not compel the Legislature to establish a preference primary, similar to those in use in several Mainland states, to express Hawaii's choice of presidential candidates to the national party convention.

A preference primary would allow the people a greater voice in the selection of party presidential candidates. The present system, where delegates are selected at state party conventions, gives the people of Hawaii little voice in picking presidential candidates.

12. MINIMUM AGE OF LEGISLATORS.

Lowers the minimum age requirement for legislators to the age of majority (20 years as set by law). Now, senators must be at least 30 and representatives 25.

Young people, as a group, should not be excluded from seeking to serve in the Legislature. They ought to be given the opportunity to run for office and have the people accept or reject them on their abilities, rather than being barred from running by an arbitrary age barrier.

13. LEGISLATIVE SESSIONS, POWERS, RIGHTS AND PROCEDURES.

Provides for annual sessions of 60 working days (12 weeks), instead of the present system of alternating 30- and 60-day sessions. Gives the Legislature power to extend its own sessions or to call special sessions. Establishes a commission to review legislators' pay periodically.

Longer annual sessions give legislators time for complete review of bills without end-of-session work jam-up. Power to extend sessions and call special sessions gives legislators more flexibility and freedom. The salary commission insures an independent review of legislators' pay.

20. COLLECTIVE BARGAINING FOR PUBLIC EMPLOYEES.

The Legislature may authorize government workers to organize and bargain collectively. Now, such employees may organize and "present grievances" to the government.

Like private workers, government employees should be able to band together to work out the details and conditions of their employment. The Legislature, by statute, will set rules concerning the extent of bargaining allowed.

21. CODES OF ETHICS AND DISQUALIFICATION FOR DISLOYALTY.

Requires that the State and each county have codes of ethics for all appointed and elected officials and employees.

Adopts a new provision prohibiting government employment for any person involved in a deliberately disloyal act or conspiracy.

Codes of ethics stress the importance of avoiding conflicts of interest and unethical conduct in government.

In line with recent court decisions, the disloyalty provision provides more specific criteria for refusing a person a government job because of disloyalty.

22. REVISIONS AND AMENDMENTS TO THE CONSTITUTION.

Provides that, unless otherwise provided by the Legislature, a future Constitutional Convention will have the same powers and privileges as the Convention of 1968.

This sets up the basic structure for a future Constitutional Convention.

23. TECHNICAL, TRANSITIONAL, STYLE AND OTHER CHANGES.

Deletions and minor changes in wording of various sections to eliminate unconstitutional portions no longer needed or since ruled unconstitutional; other changes in style.

These changes in style and wording make the Constitution internally consistent and polish the language of the document.

In order to save you some time at your polling place, we encourage you to study the Proposed Amendments to the Hawaii State Constitution ahead of time. When you have made your decisions, we recommend that you mark your choice or choices on the sample ballot (in back) and take it with you to your polling place. By following your pre-marked sample ballot as you vote, you will complete your voting sooner, thus preventing long waiting lines.

THE CONSTITUTIONAL CONVENTION OF 1968/SUBMISSION AND INFORMATION COMMITTEE

A month before the close of the convention the Committee on Submission and Information called for proposals from experts in the public information field to carry out a program for securing public approval and voter acceptance of the recommendations, providing adequate and understandable information on the issues. Proposals were to include the use of citizen groups, public service broadcasts and telecasts, as well as paid advertising. Cost was left open. After bids had been received, the committee revised plans and, in lieu of conducting the educational campaign through contract, hired a public relations expert for two months as convention public information officer.

Since the convention determined not to submit the constitutional revision at a special election, automatically, pursuant to the act setting up the convention, the proposed changes would be voted on at the general election in November 1968. This allowed only a little over a month to conduct a campaign to sell the 1968 revision. Unlike 1950, there were now adequate funds available to finance a lavish campaign, but the leadership desired to conserve funds and the staff public relations expert counseled a low-key approach which eventually cost about $40,000.

1968: The Campaign

Preparatory to undertaking the educational campaign, and in aid of the original decision on packaging the ballot, a small-scale poll was taken of Oahu voters. This disclosed that 52 percent of the sample thought the convention delegates had, in general, done a good job; only 8 percent held negative attitudes; 26 percent were undecided and 13 percent refused to respond. Forty-six percent indicated that, if the election were being held at the time they were interviewed, they would vote for the constitutional revision, and only 12 percent registered "no" votes; the balance was undecided (29 percent) or unresponsive (13 percent). Exposure to the work of the convention through the mass media had not helped determine positive or negative reactions, but lack of exposure increased the probability of indecision. Although negative responses were registered on particular issues, the generally favorable attitude indicated that the wisest course was to concentrate the greatest effort on overcoming voter inertia and influencing them to cast ballots on the revision.

Under the slogan of "Know the issues . . . then vote on the amendments to Hawaii's Constitution" an educational campaign sought to reach all voters through word of mouth, visually and in print. Pamphlets describing the proposals were made available at the primary election polling paces, distributed over the counters of financial institutions, and included in employees' pay envelopes. Advertisements covering most of a page in the daily newspapers explained the proposed changes and the reasons the delegates voted for them. Television and radio stations carried spot announcements reminding voters to cast ballots, and of their responsibility for voting intelligently. On educational television, convention delegates were featured in half-hour panels probing the reasons for actions in specific areas. An active speakers' bureau utilized the services of delegates in carrying the message to citizen groups. Throughout, the picture of an Hawaiian flag, with Island people—mainly children—striding forward under it, provided a unifying symbol for the commission's efforts, and later was even adopted by the newspapers to aid in identifying convention subjects.

Unlike 1950, no concerted effort developed to defeat the entire constitutional package. Opposition was limited to individual items, and there were no "anti-amendment" advertising campaigns reminiscent of those recently conducted to defeat constitutional change in several mainland states. The unions and the Democratic party wholeheartedly supported the revision. The business groups were less laudatory and recommended "no" votes on some of the propositions. The Republican party took a middle-of-the-road position, praising the work of the convention president (a Republican) but merely urging that citizens "study the issues." The party's state chairman, however, as an individual, joined the parade of Democratic congressional and state officeholders in publicly urging a blanket "yes" vote. Illustrative of the "reverse English" implicit in the "yes-but" portion of the ballot, the Citizens' Committee on Ethics in Government asked its members to urge their friends "not to vote 'No'" on the ethics proposal.

Writers of letters to the editor concentrated their opposition on the $12,000 annual salary for legislators, the increased public debt ceiling, elimination of the literacy provision for voters, 18-year-old voting, and collective bargaining for governmental employees. Some criticized the alleged lack of publicity on the amendments, but there was little objection that the Committee on Submission and Information was publishing only the side of the issue favorable to its position. Although one of the delegates, a Democrat running for election to the legislature, charged that the convention's reapportionment plan represented a Republican gerrymander for certain areas in Honolulu, the Democrats uniformly refuted him, defending President Porteus and the convention.

The main worry was over whether there would be too many spoiled ballots or people not bothering to vote on the constitutional issue, so as to fail to meet the requisite 35 percent figure. The committee in its advertisements never urged voters to mark the first section of their ballot (unqualified "yes") but instead stressed voting, and limited to only one of the three parts. A spoiled ballot would be included in the total count, against which the 35 percent requirement would be measured, while a vote in either the "yes" or "yes-but" portions would provide affirmative tallies toward satisfying the constitutional minimum. The League of Women Voters' pamphlet, giving the pros and cons on all 23 items, was published under a cover bearing the title "Your Vote Makes a Difference." Editorials in the public press repeated the theme that citizens should get out and vote on the convention issues. One Honolulu daily editorialized, "We strongly urge a simple 'yes' vote in section one [unqualified "yes"] . . . because of the complicated nature of this ballot there is a grave risk of unintentional mistakes in voting . . . a substantial number of errors in voting would threaten defeat of the con-con's work [due to the 35 percent qualification]. . . ."

Just before the election, an unsuccessful candidate for delegate, who had refused to file his expense account and consequently had been convicted of a misdemeanor for failure to do so, applied for an injunction before the state supreme court. He objected to the forthcoming election on the ground that the public had not been adequately informed on the proposed amendments. The court refused to interfere both because the petition was technically inadequate and because it was too close to the time of the election.

1968: The Vote

When the voters went to the polls, in most precincts they received punch-card ballots, carrying under "Part C" short titles for the 23 proposals for which they could cast a "no" vote. Available at the polls was an information booklet prepared by the lieutenant governor, containing a brief description of each ballot question and directions on how to vote the ballot. Despite instructions to the precinct workers, this was not automatically handed out to each voter, so that most went into the voting booth with only the ballot. Previously the lieutenant governor had widely distributed a sample ballot, attached to which was an explanation of the amendments prepared by the Committee on Submission and Public Information; voters were told to study this ahead of time, and then bring it with them to the polls to speed up the voting process. Should a voter have demanded to see the exact amendments on which he was being requested to cast a ballot (as this writer experimentally did), they were nowhere available in *haec verba* for his scrutiny. Just a few days before the election it had been announced that copies of the state constitution, with all proposed amendments incorporated, were available for inspection at the offices of the constitutional convention in the basement of Iolani Palace. A copy of the same sample constitution was placed at each polling booth but, on examination, it proved impossible to link the circled numbers on its margins with the precise proposals being voted on in the ballot. Most voters were not interested in ascertaining the language of each change being made in the state's fundamental law, and the few who were had to take the convention's product on faith. The latter is best illustrated by the affirmative vote received on item 23, labeled "Technical, Transitional, Style and Other Changes" on the ballot, which was in no way indicated on the sample constitution.

The ballots counted, the 1968 convention tallied an almost total record of success. One proposal only, that lowering voting age to 18, failed of passage. The backlash from the student protest in Hawaii and around the nation had contributed to the defeat. The strong antagonism to this proposal had been revealed during the post-convention period both by letters to the editor and telephone calls to the convention's office. There had been virtually no visible organized effort among young people to persuade the electorate to support the 18-year-old vote and thus counter the opposition. In all, 25,287, had voted against the constitutional revision in its entirety (Plan B), 49,546 had endorsed it en toto without any qualification (Plan A), but the success of the revision is directly attributable to the some 81,313 voters who punched "no" on at least one proposal—particularly the 56,031 "no" votes on lowering the voting age and thereby registered an affirmative vote on the balance of the proposals on which they took no action.

In retrospect, use of the "yes" by implication vote constituted a questionable practice. Many voters failed to appreciate that their voting "no" on one issue was not interpreted as being neutral on the others, but instead, automatically meant a "yes" vote on all items not singled out for separate, negative treatment. As stated to a newspaper reporter by one housewife, "I think you should have been able to vote 'yes' or 'no' after each amendment. Having parts A, B, and C was confusing . . . especially part C. I did not understand it was an automatic 'yes' for the ones you did not punch 'no.' I did not realize that until afterwards. . . . I am sure a lot of people did not. It was rigged so it would pass." Fifty-two percent of the citizens who cast ballots for the constitution did so under alternative C, emphasizing their negative choices; an additional 16 percent voted under alternative B, disapproving of the entire document.

DISTRIBUTION OF CONSTITUTIONAL VOTE 1968

Prop.	"No" Spec. (C)	All "No" (B)	Total "No"	All "Yes" (A)	"Yes" by Impl. (C)	Total "Yes"
1	10,162	25,287	35,449	49,546	71,151	120,697
2	7,069	25,287	32,356	49,546	74,244	123,790
3	11,577	25,287	36,864	49,546	69,736	119,282
4	8,432	25,287	33,719	49,546	72,881	122,427
5	8,493	25,287	33,780	49,546	67,820	117,366
6	7,980	25,287	33,267	49,546	73,333	122,879
7	7,405	25,287	32,692	49,546	74,908	123,454
8	56,031	25,287	81,318	49,546	25,282	74,828
9	28,267	25,287	53,554	49,546	53,046	102,592
10	35,531	25,287	60,818	49,546	45,782	95,328
11	12,146	25,287	37,433	49,546	69,167	118,713
12	43,647	25,287	68,934	49,546	37,467	87,013
13	10,810	25,287	36,097	49,546	71,503	120,049
14	42,523	25,287	67,810	49,546	38,790	88,336
15	24,443	25,287	49,730	49,546	56,870	106,416
16	12,775	25,287	38,062	49,546	68,538	118,084
17	17,874	25,287	43,161	49,546	63,439	112,985
18	10,771	25,287	36,058	49,546	70,942	120,488
19	5,730	25,287	31,017	49,546	75,583	125,129
20	24,600	25,287	49,887	49,546	56,713	106,259
21	6,255	25,287	31,542	49,546	75,058	124,604
22	6,639	25,287	31,926	49,546	74,674	124,220
23	6,344	25,287	31,631	49,546	74,969	124,515

Thirty-two percent voted "yes" under alternative A, supporting the entire constitution.

The "yes by implication" vote registered on 18 issues was greater than the sum of both the specific "no" vote on the proposal and the general "no" vote on the entire ballot. In addition, it was also larger than the express "yes" vote. All these data evidence the importance of the citizen having voted against some other issue. It is true that in 16 proposals the express "yes" votes outnumbered all the "no" votes, so that for each of these a majority of the citizens voting on them indicated approval. But that is not the only criterion raised by Hawaii's constitution. At the general election in 1968, 239,765 votes were cast, and none of the 23 issues received a positive "yes" vote equalling 35 percent of this amount. It was only the "yes by implication" procedure which saved them. Given the voters' trenchant to single out a few salient issues and remain silent on the balance, had Hawaii followed the normal practice of a "yes" or "no" vote on each of the 23 proposals, more issues than the 18-year-old minimum voting age would have been defeated. How many would have failed due to voter inaction, thus running afoul of the 35 percent criterion, must always remain conjecture, but as many as three more might have died as a result of outright voter rejection.

Of the seven issues in which the total "no" vote tallied more than the express "yes," only one was defeated. For three the spread was sizable enough to suggest that they might have been rejected on a straight "yes-no" vote:

ISSUES ON WHICH "NO" VOTE EXCEEDED EXPRESS "YES"

Issue	Total "No"	Express "Yes"	Difference
8. 18-year-old vote	81,318	49,546	(defeated)
9. Felon voting right	53,554	49,546	4,008
10. Literacy requirement	60,818	49,546	11,272
12. Age of legislators	68,934	49,546	19,388
14. Legislator comp.	67,810	49,546	18,264
15. Eligibility of Gover.	49,730	49,546	184
20. Collective Bargaining	49,887	49,546	341

At the pre-election poll, issues 8, 10 and 14 revealed sizable negative sentiment; for both issues 9 and 20, stronger support was evident. Queries were not raised as to the other two, but given the large negative vote cast on issue 12 (reduction in age of legislators), it might well have gone down to defeat with the legislative compensation issue (14) and

elimination of the literacy requirement (10) if only "yes" and "no" votes
were recorded.

PRE-ELECTION POLL OF OAHU VOTER SAMPLE

Issue	Yes	No	D.N.	N.R.
8. Extend vote to 18-year-olds	35%	35%	17%	13%
9. Right to vote to felons	47	18	21	13
10. Abolish literacy requirement	28	35	25	13
14. Legislative compensation ($12,000)	19	44	24	14
20. Collective bargaining	37	23	27	13

D.N. = "Don't Know" response. N.R. = "No Response" to question.

From the vantage point of achievement, the convention had remark-
able success in "selling" its product. Even the one issue which was defeated represented only a temporary rejection, for the next legislative
session returned it to the voters for another chance at ratification. The
ethics of using the appeal of statehood in 1950 to swamp the objectors
to the proposed state constitution may be debated with little chance of
resolution. The question of whether the means are ever justified by the
end, however, was dramatically raised at the 1968 elections. The "yes-
but" portion of the ballot was indeed effective, but was it moral?

10.

The Convention Appraised

Disbanded, its recommendations ratified at the polls, the repercussions from the convention lingered on. In individual perspective, each delegate's participation potentially influenced his own future; some were catapulted to positions of prominence which augured well for subsequent political careers. The 1950 constitution was the signal for applying renewed vigor in the statehood drive; the 1968 modifications constituted commands to the three branches of the state government to undertake their implementation. And for the scholar it now became possible to view the convention in perspective, analyzing its process and product, and subjecting it to normative appraisal.

The post-convention impact in 1968 was immediate in both personal and institutional terms. Right after the convention closed, more than half of the 82 delegates ran for office at the primary election. Of the 44 who sought nomination, 33 were successful. Institutionally, to comply with the new constitutional mandates some statutory changes were essential at the forthcoming legislative session, while other constitutional directives could be promptly instituted through administrative action. In addition, many statutes were impliedly amended or repealed by the constitutional changes, so that, if not immediately, at least in the near future their language would have to be revised in order to bring them into conformance with the constitution. Thus the dropping of the literacy requirement made the voter registration affidavit obsolete, and the raising of the state and county debt ceilings necessitated extensive correctional revisions in the applicable statutes. And there were also the constitutional changes which called for new commissions and provided for future action, which could be delayed, but not beyond the time limits set by the constitution or dictated by political pressures.

New Legislative Directions

The new directions in the legislative article for a 24-hour delay in the final passage of legislation and for the carry-over of bills from one session to another required only minor modification of the legislative standing rules, and proved non-controversial. In contrast the scaling down of the legislative per diem to be reasonably related to actual expenses became the center of contention in a protracted struggle between the two houses over the appropriation necessary to run the 1969 legislature. The constitutional changes which eliminated the staggering of Senate terms and had all legislators running for office in 1970 encouraged this early jockeying for position by incumbents and helped explain the adamant stand of each house. Other appropriations were also directly affected, such as the $500,000 request by the governor to meet the cost of providing counsel to indigents in misdemeanor cases, now that the constitution declares their right to such assistance.

Where immediate action was not imperative, interim committees could be assigned the duty of studying and reporting on steps to be taken, and this promptly occurred. In some cases, such as that relating to collective bargaining for public employees "as prescribed by law," enactment of the necessary enabling legislation was delayed until the issue could be politically defused, or at least all alternatives carefully explored and a politically defensible course charted. Undoubtedly, for years to come, the legislature will have to give considerable part of its attention to making technical changes and responding to the new constitutional mandates whose implementation depends on statute.

Neighbor Island—Oahu Dichtomy

In retrospect, it is now apparent that the 1968 convention could have split dysfunctionally along two lines, one of them attributable to Neighbor Islands-Oahu disparity. Early, the selection of officers and the convention's seating pattern reflected this dichotomy. In electing vice presidents the Neighbor Island delegations first agreed on their choices and these delegates made the nominating and closing speeches. Once committee assignments were announced, switching by delegates was declared possible only within county delegations. Neighbor Island delegates were seated in county groupings on one side of the convention floor, separately from their Oahu colleagues, rather than mixed indiscriminately or assigned seats in alphabetical order. This physical contiguity possibly encouraged some of the Neighbor Island delegates occasionally to engage in clowning antics, and further set them apart.

The delegates from the Neighbor Islands displayed a sense of group solidarity throughout the convention. They expected distinctive recognition for themselves and their counties, and used their cohesiveness advantage toward that end. Viewed against the majority strength which theoretically Oahu could muster within the convention, in general the Neighbor Islanders anticipated and received more considerate treatment than warranted when measured by the city and county's overwhelming weight of population, wealth and greater complexity of problems.

The trips scheduled for the delegates to the various islands permitted a degree of liaison between their people and the convention. Of course, Oahu constituents enjoyed far greater opportunity to make personal contact with their delegates, should they have desired to do so. A good deal of formalism underlay much of this Neighbor Island visitation, constituting an attempt to legitimize the actions of the convention, to anticipate and neutralize any Neighbor Island objection to the finished product.

In a number of policy decisions the final choice of the convention was more favorable to the Neighbor Islands than if a competing alternative had been selected. "Registered voters" as the base for apportionment was to the relative disadvantage of Oahu, as the other islands enjoy a higher rate of registration. The defeat of the "merit plan" for selection of judges removed the potential danger that Oahu lawyers would dictate the naming of Neighbor Island judges. Issues could not be neatly categorized along geographical lines, however, and delegates similarly did not align themselves. If anything revealed a disparity of view between Oahu and the Neighbor Islands, it was over increasing the powers of local government, with the officers of the latter giving nominal support to the city and county spearheading the drive. But then, many Oahu delegates did not favor this proposed reversal of the long-time Island pattern of centralization, so that the issue could hardly be classified as revealing a fundamental geographical dichotomy. It was tacitly accepted as only proper for Neighbor Island delegates to tend to matters pertaining to their own areas, such as legislative districting, and that, when they could reach consensus, to respect their agreements. On the other hand, Neighbor Island delegates did not hesitate to participate in matters relating to Oahu, and again this was regarded as only natural, given the colossus which is the city and county of Honolulu.

Legislators and Non-Legislators

The other schism which was early anticipated would have pitted delegates with legislative experience against non-legislators in the convention. The former having majority strength and greater knowledge of the intricacies of parliamentary maneuver, presumably they would have emerged victorious in any such contest. The protest voiced after so many incumbent legislators declared their candidacy appeared to presage a sharply bifurcated convention, once the elections were concluded. That the cleavage failed to develop was initially due to the steps taken to assuage the fears of "non-professionals" prior to the convention, and principally because the legislators mounted no concerted effort toward directing the course of the convention. Unlike the 1950 convention, few sought or achieved any unusual saliency on the convention floor. Legislator-delegates from Oahu, the island on which pre-election criticism had been heaviest, particularly understood that they would escape public opprobrium by following this strategy, which of course did not prevent them from seeking to influence the deliberations and decisions of the constitutional convention when they so desired.

Although a senator, the choice of Hebden Porteus as convention president followed his public commitment to an open convention without the imposition of legislative-type constraints on convention procedure or an inner cabal to direct policy. The proposal for eight vice presidents which was raised in caucus would have incorporated senatorial structure into the convention; its defeat in part reflected the delegates' desire to have a convention without such direct institutional parallelism. (Nevertheless, with the officers all elected, their geographical distribution accorded with the state's senatorial apportionment!) The inclusion of non-legislators among the officers symbolized that control was not being surrendered to the legislator-delegates. No attempt was made either to introduce the legislative floor organization or to conform convention procedures closely to the legislative model. Serving as a capstone, President Porteus's committee assignments placed non-legislators in the politically most important chairmen posts, and carefully divided committee membership so that legislator domination was not possible. The one exception—the composition of the rules committee—drew no objection. The anxiety of the non-legislators which was countered by these various moves further subsided as the legislator-delegate bloc made no move to exert institutional leadership. Concomitantly, as non-legislators experienced the inertia of getting convention business under way, they began to appreciate the value of legislative experience in overcoming some procedural and substantive difficulties. There was a slight resurgence of apprehension as the convention went into Committee of the Whole and legislators were appointed the initial chairmen, but they were soon followed by the designation of non-legislators. The legislators' inclination to speed the work of the convention, and the impatience which many solons exhibited contributed to keeping alive a residuum of suspicion. This, and the fact that some opposition to legislator participation in any constitutional convention continued to be publicly voiced, assured that such leadership as most legislator-delegates did exercise would have low visibility.

None of the foregoing negates the noticeable differences between legislator and non-legislator-delegates at the 1968 convention. As "non-professionals" the latter had to learn how to disport themselves in a collegial body; the former had established roles in the legislature and, insofar as applicable, they tended to carry over into the convention. Some with many years of legislative training enjoyed considerable advantage by virtue of their familiarity with parliamentary procedure as well as subject matter areas certain to come before the convention. At the outset, inexperienced committee chairmen consulted their legislator-delegate colleagues and borrowed widely from the committee rules drafted by them, this after the president had rejected a request to circulate a set of model committee rules for the use of all convention committees.

As procedural problems arose in the convention, legislator-delegates were quick to offer suggestions for solution, while delegates without legislative experience characteristically were inclined to approach the difficulty by first asking clarifying questions. On proposals directed to the legislative article, whether concerned with structural or procedural change, delegates with legislative experience could speak from first-hand knowledge, taking positions which the non-legislator found difficult to counter. When disagreement arose over legislative amendments, it normally was between legislators. Legislators were also more factually informed on the "sensitive" issues, and on the political nuances of all issues of which the other delegates were sometimes not even aware.

Legislator-delegates appeared more jealous of their own committee's area of jurisdiction, and prone to contest the "poaching" of committees with overlapping responsibilities. This was but one manifestation of the difference in general attitude which they brought to their committee assignments. More so than the non-legislator, they appreciated that an expert witness was not necessarily a generalist knowledgeable on the whole subject matter under consideration, and that his creditability was not destroyed by responses revealing narrow specialization. They were also more inclined to accept a witness's critical comments as a personal affront, and were particularly sensitive to any disparagement of the legislative institution. And, of course, the legislator-delegate could always warn a witness that his testimony was not consistent with a position previously taken before the legislature, and threaten to open the entire matter for review at the next legislative session.

Legislators displayed little reluctance to participate actively in debate where conflict of interest could arise, such as consideration of increases in their own salaries. Contrary to what might be expected, they were far from unanimous in pushing for expansion of legislative powers, although it ought to be added that several delegates taking the strongest positions contrary to legislative aggrandizement had no intention to run for reelection. Legislator-delegates also split over other substantive changes; here, differences of position within the legislative chambers frequently carried over to advocacy in the convention, including overtones of long-standing personality clashes. As might be anticipated, legislator-delegates were in the forefront of opposition to the projected decentralization of power to the counties, and to the incorporation into the constitution of a strong code of ethics. That proposals relating to both were finally approved by the convention does not testify to the defeat of the legislator-delegate, for these amendments were adopted only after being drastically weakened, and may prove to represent hollow victories.

Convention and Legislature

The variances in behavior noted between the legislator and non-legislator delegate at the 1968 convention touch on the distinctive difference between the legislature and the constitutional convention. Both are legislative bodies in view of their representative nature and their use of collegial processes, and both are concerned with lawmaking. But there the dualism ends, for the constitutional convention embodies many institutional characteristics attributable to its ad hoc nature and more fundamental functions which distinguish it from a legislature. A convention begins to approximate a legislature both in process and product only as these differences are negated. This distinction was sensed by many delegates at the 1968 convention, but never fully articulated, and led some dissatisfied delegates who had also served in the statehood convention to draw unflattering comparisons between the two.

The sub-system called a legislature embodies a reciprocal mix of politicized legislators, bureaucratized staff, routinized procedures, and complementary setting of individual constituents and organized groups involved to some degree in affecting legislative decisions. Even though a constitutional convention may borrow superficially from legislative practice, such as calling the 1968 convention to order by the delegate elected from the 1st representative district in imitation of the Hawaiian legislature, this does not make it a legislative body. Nor does the fact that the convention uses novel procedures—as the committees in Hawaii's 1968 convention sometimes deciding by plurality among three or more alternatives, rather than by "either-or" majority vote—necessarily testify to a convention being fundamentally different from a legislature. It is a matter of holistic comparison of the constitutional convention with the entire, interrelated legislative complex.

This may be illustrated by the orientation process at the 1968 convention. There was no indoctrination of the neophyte delegate by the "professional" to the established formalities and folkways, but a mutual development of procedures by which the new body was to be run. In committee, there was first a joint exploration of subject matter until all delegates were (presumably) able to turn to the resolution of specific problems. There was no pre-existing hierarchy of position with which the newcomer had to familiarize himself at his own peril. Lobbyists, too, had to learn how to make contact with an entirely amorphous body. All—delegates, staff, constituents—were being introduced to a new institution for which history offered some precepts and paralleling institutions some useful practices, but in which respective roles had to evolve *ab initio*.

As head of a collegial body without direct antecedents, both in 1950 and in 1968 the presidents furnished leadership through the persuasiveness of their logic and demonstrated parliamentary innovativeness. This contrasts with an established legislature where rote observance of folkways, covert aid of an inner group or open support of the majority political party organization may be sufficient to gloss over the presiding officer's personality or parliamentary deficiencies. Indeed, since all institutionalized leadership patterns were ill-defined, the president's skills assumed convention-wide importance, resulting in his taking a major part in a broad range of procedural matters, such as in the Committee of the Whole where others presided. Similarly, each committee chairman initially assumed his position in the convention as one among equals, armed only with power over staff, agenda and designation by the president as presiding officer; he enjoyed no powers of seniority or ties to either formal or informal institutional power structure, and he developed his office as befitted his own abilities and imposed convention responsibilities.

In contrast with the introduction of bills on the legislative scene, the individual delegate stood to gain little political advantage from sponsoring proposals in the convention. At time of presentation, the mass media might mention the delegate, but thereafter the proposals passed into near oblivion with only the convention index and status table publicly continuing to identify them and to indicate their last resting place. When the convention attorneys prepared a digest of a proposal, it was designed for use by and distributed to the committee considering it, so that the delegate did not obtain the benefit of even this minimal form of convention-wide recognition. In effect, once referred, the delegate's proposals disappeared in committee, later to be returned to the convention and filed. If embodied in a committee proposal, no individual delegate's name ever became associated; not even the chairman's name was attached to the committee proposal.

In a legislature, the individual member maneuvers for passage of legislation he favors through mustering a maximum of strength on its behalf. To that end he may engage in trading votes, linking the fate of measures, enlist the internal power structure's support, appeal to external sources for pressuring the legislature, or employ other similar devices. Few parallels were encountered in the constitutional convention of 1968. Neither individual delegates nor committee chairmen were in a position to tie together the fate of proposals, and the convention's more fluid structure and the limited sanctions of its formal leadership discouraged attempts at trading or otherwise lining up support. In truth there was very little for a delegate to trade other than his one vote plus such following as his persuasive powers might enlist; occasionally outside "currency" could be added, such as promise of backing in some future political undertaking. No wonder that some lobbyists experienced in legislative service objected to working with the convention, given the difficulties of identifying boundaries for permissible negotiation, the ill-defined leadership structure, and the absence of means for securing any commitment. All of this contributed to lower-keyed political activity, with delegates as a whole having less occasion to seek out or take advantage of political opportunities as they might arise; those delegates who did capitalize on the political potential of the convention stood out conspicuously from their colleagues.

Unlike the *pro forma* nature of normal legislative debate, with major deliberation occurring in committee or within the confines of the legislature's policy group, so that floor action is fundamentally little more than a routinized recording of votes, the conventions gave extended consideration to each committee proposal. More so in 1950 than in 1968, the delegates did not hesitate to attempt a major revision of a committee proposal; in both conventions there was no reluctance to question and debate standing committee decisions. Except for the membership of the committee which originally studied a proposal, most of the remaining delegates came to the issue uncommitted. All delegates had full opportunity to participate. As one consequence, delegates were visibly attentive to proceedings on the convention floor, and this not only when they were being televised, as some of the critics of the convention's TV coverage derogatively charged. Floor debate must be counted as an important factor in shaping the final convention product.

The convention also disclosed itself more willing than a legislature to reconsider decisions once made. Charged with matters of fundamental nature, delegates did not take their responsibility lightly, and were not disinclined to cover the same ground again on the chance that error may have been committed. Unlike legislators, once their task was completed the delegates would have no subsequent opportunity to rectify their mistakes. Individually and collectively, deliberation was the rule and caution was the guiding standard. Sometimes this was revealed in the convention's readiness to adjourn in order to permit delegates greater time for reflection; other times it found form in failure to take any action at all. Lacking internal leadership committed in advance to specific policy, devoid of an executive branch advocating programmatic objectives and continuously impinging from the outside, and apparently numbering within its membership few delegates whose own political advancement hinged on demonstrated ability to move the convention toward achieving certain pre-determined goals, the convention was in position to realize its full potential as a deliberative body charged with the identification and resolution of fundamental matters in a manner designed to further broad community welfare.

Like legislators, delegates were faced with the dilemma of representation. Given the subject matter of their actions and the limited communication of constituent concern, initially it was easy for the convention delegates to profess the role of trustee, declaring that they were elected to do what they thought best for the state rather than merely to act as spokesmen for their constituents' views. Moreover, it was safe for them to do so, as the manner in which they met the problem of representation would be impersonally tested at the polls, with the convention rather than individuals bearing the burden of voter disapproval. Few suffered any major risk to their political ambitions should the voters refuse to ratify the proposed constitutional amendments when submitted. That the delegates did not tend to hold to a trustee role, but were willing to modify their position as the convention moved to final decision, arose from the necessity of the convention's securing popular consent for its proposals, so that each change had to be cut to the measure of the politically feasible. In addition, the greater the show of solidarity displayed by the delegates, the more the voters might be influenced to accept the convention's decision. This led the delegates to act more on the plane of the possible (that is, as a politico) than on that of theoretical abstraction with its bipolarization between trustee and spokesman. Debate in Committee of the Whole might be sharp, and the vote on an amendment nearly evenly divided, but final adoption on the convention floor with its roll call vote found the delegates closing ranks, with near unanimity recorded. However he might have classified if systematically interviewed through use of hypothetical questions on style of representation, as legislators have been, the convention delegate was in a position to be influenced more by the risk of jeopardizing the success of the convention's work than by any constituent reaction to himself, and he responded by tending to act as political realist.

To facilitate deliberation and the exercise of caution, a series of time-lags was deliberately built into the procedures of both the 1950 and 1968 conventions. The four-day minimum gap separating the printing of committee proposals from the opening of Committee of the Whole debates; the foregoing of guillotine motions during the Committee of the Whole; the requirement for the printing of all floor amendments before their consideration; the further delay to second reading after the Committee of the Whole reported and then the possibility of once again covering the same ground during the second reading debate; the two reviews by the Style Committee, once before and again after third reading; the 48-hour delay before third reading—these and comparable provisions were all designed to denigrate the importance of speed. Complementing this, it was well understood that, within the strictures of a legislature's periodic session, little opportunity is afforded to plumb beneath the superficial into fundamentals, so the conventions' charters avoided all reference to limitations on their length of life. Unlike the statehood convention, however, the 1968 convention was held under restrictive handicaps which greatly neutralized the effect of all these safeguards.

The pressure exerted on the delegates to complete their work resulted in the 1968 convention being skewed toward an emphasis on speed, all with a view to adjourning within a fixed deadline. The convening date set by the legislature practically gave it a maximum operational life of two and a half months, or at best it would then have to recess for the state's primary election early in October and continue inactive until after the general election in November. The choice of a school as the convention site, which had to be vacated by September, daily communicated to the delegates that speed was essential. From the very outset, non-legislators reported subtle pressure from legislator-delegates to move the work of the convention along; as the convention continued the subtlety disappeared.

One of the recurring themes in the speeches delivered during the convening ceremonies was for an "expeditious convention." When it became apparent that the convention was not to wind up its affairs by the end of August, some delegates began campaigning actively for elective office, and this only exacerbated the tension. The president publicly refused to apply a gag on debate or fix a deadline for session termination, but the committee chairmen were led to understand that the pace of the convention's work must be quickened and the committees pushed to decision making. Once the first standing committee proposal was reported out for the second reading, Committee of the Whole and plenary meetings began preempting the convention's working day, so that the standing committees were under additional compulsion to conclude their deliberations. Toward the end of the convention, pressure for speed increased to the point of parliamentary waivers of some of the rules initially adopted to slow down convention action. With resolutions in the Rules Committee on shortening debate as well as truncating the life of the convention itself, delegates who might have been otherwise disposed responded to the threat by foregoing the unique opportunity afforded by the calling of a convention, time for appraisal of fundamentals, and then consideration of the specifics incorporated into the constitution.

The Media and the Convention

The mass media failed to make the citizen aware of the fact that the 1968 convention had insufficient time to come to grips with matters basic to the body politic, for they were too busy popularizing the convention and its product. Initially they helped involve citizens in constitution making by encouraging candidates to file and registered voters to go to the polls at the special convention election. Later they kept the public informed concerning the conferences and caucuses which preceded the convening, and about the daily activities of the convention. Frequently they voluntarily facilitated the work of the convention by carrying announcements of meetings and otherwise communicating convention requests. In their reporting they took great pains to make interesting much which would by its subject matter nature be dull and devoid of any attraction to the average citizen. The work of the convention concluded, the newspapers editorially endorsed the convention's amendments, and recommended their approval, which undoubtedly contributed to their acceptance. Given the mass media's generally critical attitude toward the legislature, the favorable approach they adopted toward the convention assumes added dimension.

A constitutional convention normally is a commendable civic undertaking, and while there was some disagreement in Hawaii over whether one was warranted in 1968, once it was decided it should be held, an expression of appreciation is due the mass media for their general supportive efforts. This, however, does not erase the disservice which was also inherent in the way that support was rendered. The reporters and commentators were so busy in aid of "good government" that they either unconsciously ignored weaknesses of the convention, or deliberately avoided referring to them in order not to discredit the delegates and thereby run the risk of the voters becoming alienated. Whatever the cause, the citizens of Hawaii were not furnished with equal treatment of the convention's negative aspects. This might have led to a less favorable public image, but would also have assured that even "good government" is held accountable for its inadequacies.

Editorials which appeared in both of Honolulu's daily newspapers proposed the gauge for evaluating the work of the 1968 constitutional convention. The checklist carried by the *Honolulu Star-Bulletin* on July 15, while embodying certain specific policy preferences of the editor, also serves to indicate the general tenor of the standards employed by the mass media for judging the convention:

1. Did it proceed expeditiously?

2. Did it carefully review the entire Constitution?

3. Did it give a fair hearing to all? Did it operate openly and democratically?

4. Did it adhere to the dictum of seeking a minimum number of changes, rather than a maximum, recognizing that the present document is basically good?

5. Did it submit its proposed changes to the public in a meaningful way, subdividing these for separate acceptance or rejection on a reasonable basis?

6. Did it conscientiously review the question of legislative structure and apportionment? Did non-legislators assert the initiative in this area against the inevitable self-interest of legislative members in the status quo?

7. Did it give careful review to the judicial article and seek meaningful improvements in our methods of selecting and removing judges (both are important) and study the kind of tenure rules that will give us a qualified and independent judiciary?

8. Did it study the status of the Board of Education which now seems neither fish nor fowl in the government structure—with an autonomous elected board at its head but no tax or fund-raising powers by which it can function independently?

9. Did it improve the outdated article on debt limit?

10. Do its final proposals help us toward a better Hawaii?

When the work of the convention was completed, the editor publicly concluded on September 23 that the convention deserved a "yes" answer to all of the questions, and that ". . . the first overhaul of our Constitution since 1950 has proven useful and fruitful."

What is partially expressed and wholly consonant with this editorial is total satisfaction with the vast bulk of the constitution, and the absence of any recognition of the constitutional convention as a periodic institution charged with the duty of subjecting the state's basic law to fundamental scrutiny and reconsideration. Hawaii has long enjoyed the accolade of having an excellent state constitution, but, as one delegate expressed in his objection to the convention's speed-up, it is good because of its brief, concise language, and the absence of detail that properly belongs to a state legislature and to county legislative bodies. The same could still be said if far different provisions on specific subjects were written into the constitution.

Practicality vs. Philosophy

In retrospect, it is difficult to conclude other than that, in the main, the approach of the 1968 convention was superficial, dictated by the practical need to complete its deliberations within an insufficient span of time. Then, too, most delegates were not disposed to give attention to "philosophical" questions, and were quite content to limit themselves to those structural and functional adjustments obviously necessitated by the passage of time and the United States Supreme Court decisions. The entire argument over adoption of the "merit plan" for the designation of judges failed ever to touch on the essence of the judicial function, and whether Hawaii's court system is adequate to the needs of the present society and will continue to be for those of the anticipated future. The delegates completely ignored the warning of mainland experience with the decay of the city and the alienation of urban populations, and gave little attention to establishing a system of local government which might avoid duplication of this scourge in Hawaii. There was no interest in exploring the structuring of a new representational system, now that the federal courts have made all factors but population of secondary importance; the proposal for fractional county representation constituted not so much a breakthrough as an attempt to maintain the proscribed status quo. The tolling of the list could be further extenuated, but elaboration would only be repetitious of the same theme.

The convention which met in 1950 was primarily concerned with achieving statehood, and understood that adapting over the existing territorial structure and processes of government with minimal change for use by the state would facilitate this goal. The convention which met in 1968 was similarly uninterested in probing the basic polity and then proposing corrective revision. Just as in 1950, the delegates were disposed toward minimal, incremental change, and the convention product was of the pruning and grafting variety. Granted that its actions are only recommendatory, may not the constitutional revision commission—rather than the constitutional convention—offer greater promise for periodically undertaking fundamental study of the ills of the body politic and then proposing constitutional changes to head off catastrophic conflict before it occurs? At least, the two state conventions which have met in Hawaii lend support to that conclusion.